PRAISE FOR
P413

"This book separates itself from many others when it asks the question, 'Does the Bible promote success?' and answers with 'The Bible promotes God!'

"This book is beneficial to anyone willing to trust God for great things while holding true to the context and teaching of His word."

—John W. Gray Jr., Executive Director, The Union Mission Ministries, Norfolk Virginia

"Todd's book is a treasure trove of stories and applications that will encourage and inspire you to be the best 'you' you can be in Christ. His section on responsibility is one of the best I have read anywhere and is spot on for the serious Christ follower. Todd has succeeded in refocusing the positive-mental-attitude self-help material to where it should be—on Christ, in Christ, and about Christ."

—Dr. Donald Lynn Hardaway, Network Missionary, The Bridge Network of Churches

"*The Can-Do Code for Success and Life* is tailor made for the reader who is striving to reach their full God-given potential! This book gives clear instructions on how to go about not just talking the talk, but walking the walk as your steps are ordered by the Holy Spirit. I certainly encourage all who are in Christian leadership to read this book and share it with all those under their tutelage. I've known Dr. Holt for many years, and he is truly a shining example of what he shares in this wonderful tool for growing in one's faith!"

> —Michael Burbage, Regional Coordinator, Young Life Multiethnic

"*P413* is a great book of inspiration with a strong Christian underpinning. Through many personal experiences, pastoral examples, and biblical references, Todd has done an excellent job revealing how he and many others overcame challenges. His faith and belief in God inspires all of us to do better, be better, and reach our goals."

> —Howard Prager, Author of *Make Someone's Day: Becoming a Memorable Leader in Work and Life*, Chair, Walk of Faith and Religious Relations Committee, Northeast Illinois Council BSA

P413: The Can-Do Code for Success and Life
by K. Todd Holt

© Copyright 2023 K. Todd Holt

ISBN 979-8-88824-039-7

All rights reserved. No part of this publication may be reproduced, stored in a retrieval system, or transmitted in any form or by any means—electronic, mechanical, photocopy, recording, or any other—except for brief quotations in printed reviews, without the prior written permission of the author.

Scripture quotations are from the ESV® Bible (The Holy Bible, English Standard Version®), copyright © 2001 by Crossway, a publishing ministry of Good News Publishers. Used by permission. All rights reserved. The ESV text may not be quoted in any publication made available to the public by a Creative Commons license. The ESV may not be translated in whole or in part into any other language.

Scripture taken from the New King James Version®. Copyright © 1982 by Thomas Nelson. Used by permission. All rights reserved.

Scripture quotations taken from the (NASB) New American Standard Bible®, Copyright© 1960, 1971, 1977, 1995, 2020 by The Lockman Foundation. Used by permission. All rights reserved. Lockman.org

The author's intent of this book is only to offer information of a general nature in your quest to grow spiritually. In the event you use the information in this book, the author assumes no responsibility for your actions.

Any reference to website addresses or company or product information printed in this book are used as a resource and are not intended as an endorsement by the author or publisher.

The author is not responsible for websites (or their content).

Published by

3705 Shore Drive
Virginia Beach, VA 23455
800-435-4811
www.koehlerbooks.com

The Can-Do Code for Success and Life

K. TODD HOLT

VIRGINIA BEACH
CAPE CHARLES

*To my wife, Carol,
without whose love and support this book
would not be possible*

TABLE OF CONTENTS

Introduction 4

Section 1: Foundational Concepts for
Understanding Philippians 4:13 7

    Chapter 1: Debunk the Dunk:
    The Meaning of the Verse 8

    Chapter 2: Something Better than Self-Help 14

    Chapter 3: Blessed Burgers: The Definition of
    and Desire for Success 21

    Chapter 4: God's Love Is Better than Self-Love 32

Section 2: "I" 41

    Chapter 5: Fat-inization 42

    Chapter 6: Dative Case 55

    Chapter 7: Choose Your Hard 62

    Chapter 8: How to Become a Responsible Person ... 73

    Chapter 9: Truing the Life Wheel 79

Section 3: "CAN" 95

    Chapter 10: Everyone Has It;
    Some Know It and Grow It 96

    Chapter 11: Salvation Vacation 113

    Chapter 12: Drunk Monkeys 123

Section 4: "DO" 141

    Chapter 13: Lights, Camera, Action:
    Take Action and Start Doing 142

    Chapter 14: SMARTER: Use the SMARTER
    Goal-Setting Method for Taking Action 156

Section 5: "ALL THINGS" 175

    Chapter 15: Urim and Thummim:
    How to Discover God's Will for Your Life 176

    Chapter 16: SHAPE 197

Section 6: "THROUGH CHRIST" 211

    Chapter 17: Abiding in Christ 212

    Chapter 18: Living Water 221

Section 7: "WHO STRENGTHENS ME" 235

    Chapter 19: Ziklag 236

    Chapter 20: Rebar 250

Epilogue 269

References 270

INTRODUCTION

Many people have never realized their purpose in life, which is to love God, obey him, and seek to reach their God-given potential through Christ. This book seeks to provide help and a plan to get there, based on the Bible. The book of Philippians will serve as a guide, and a very familiar verse from the book will be our focus: Philippians 4:13.

Philippians 4:13 is printed on church signs, wall art, coffee mugs, key chains, cell phone covers, T-shirts, shoes, socks, and Bible covers. It is quoted by athletes before a game, actors auditioning for a part, students preparing for a test, as well as preachers on Saturday night. It is recited by the bravehearted who want to soar higher, as well as the brokenhearted who don't believe they can rise again.

MMA fighter John "Bones" Jones has it tattooed on his chest. Former NFL quarterback Tim Tebow wore it on his eye black. NBA star Stephen Curry wears it on his shoes. Steven Curtis Chapman sings about it. Actor Chris Pratt relies on it for strength. Professional surfer Bethany Hamilton quoted the verse while in the hospital recovering from a shark attack; she believed the verse gave her the contentment to trust the sovereignty of God in having her arm amputated. The promise of the verse also compelled her to believe in the power of Christ and continue competitive surfing.

Taken in context, and sometimes out of context, Philippians 4:13 has given faith to the timid, power to the weak, hope to the despairing, and confidence to the insecure. Because of the efficacy of its truth, many under the stress and duress of a heavy load have been given strength. For others, it has been a catalyst motivating them to attempt things they never believed they could do on their own.

"I can do all things through Christ who strengthens me" is a call to strive for more. It is a call to launch out into the deep water while keeping our eyes on Jesus. It is a call to stretch out the withered hand to be made whole. The verse is also a word of comfort in knowing God is with us when we suffer loss and failure or come up short in the pursuit of our dreams.

It is true that most new start-up companies fail. Almost 90 percent of churches are plateaued or declining. Most new wonder drugs never make it through clinical trials. Many marriages fail. Yes, life is hard! But should we not encourage the dreamer to go for it anyway? Don't we root for the underdog? Don't we long to see the hero overcome the odds?

Some Christians don't believe God has plans he wants them to pursue. Others are afraid to act on the impulse of the Holy Spirit leading them. This book seeks to encourage us to action with practical steps to reach the "all things" God has for us. In addition to the content of each chapter, I have included a "Can Do; Go Do" section that contains a couple of thought starters for taking action. It is a full circle approach to learning and doing.

Have you ever felt that God had more in store for you? That maybe God is doing a "new thing" with your name on it? Do you think that God has given you a few more "talents" to investigate before he comes (Matthew 25:14–30)? I think he does! Let the information in this book encourage you to reach your full potential through Christ.

SECTION 1

FOUNDATIONAL CONCEPTS FOR
UNDERSTANDING PHILIPPIANS 4:13

CHAPTER 1

DEBUNK THE DUNK: THE MEANING OF THE VERSE

"I can do all things through Christ who strengthens me."

PHILIPPIANS 4:13

The context in which the book of Philippians was written can help us understand the verse. At the time of writing the book of Philippians, the apostle Paul was materially destitute and in prison for preaching the gospel (Philippians 1:13). The city of Philippi was colonized by the Romans and enjoyed wealth and prestige. Luke, the writer of Acts, referred to Philippi as "the foremost city of that part of Macedonia" (Acts 16:12). Philippi was the first church Paul founded in Europe (Acts 16:6–40). Lydia, a business owner who sold purple cloth, was the first convert and played an important role in the church (Acts 16:14). During Paul's initial visit to the city, he and his fellow disciple, Silas, were imprisoned for "troubling" the city by teaching the gospel (Acts 16:20).

The church at Philippi took up a financial collection and sent it to Paul by way of Epaphroditus, a leader in the church. While with Paul, Epaphroditus became deathly ill, and God healed him. In part, the letter to the Philippians served as a thank-you note from Paul to the church for giving him financial assistance, as well as to share the news of Epaphroditus's sickness and recovery (Philippians 2:25–30). And, of course, the letter is full of encouragement and sound doctrine!

Elaborating on his situation, Paul explains in the passage that he has learned that whatever circumstances he is in, whether possessing a lot or a little, bound or free, brought low or lifted up, Christ will give him the inner strength to bear his circumstances in peace (Philippians 4:10–14). The context of the passage describes how God empowers us to live victoriously in prosperous times and during the difficulties of life.

PROMISE IN PURSUIT

What is the meaning of Philippians 4:13? Is it scriptural confirmation that good things will materialize in our lives if we think about them long enough? No. God is not forced to shift the universe to cause things to be drawn to us. We don't attract things like iron to a magnet just because we want them.

The notion that this verse is a carte blanche statement to do and get whatever one desires is falsely focused on gratifying fleshly desires rather than experiencing a deeper desire for God. Self-gratification is wide of the mark and does not take into account the context of the passage. This verse is not a guarantee we can do anything *we* want. It is a promise that God will give us the grace and ability to live victoriously, in good times and bad times, while pursuing everything *he* has in store for us.

The Passage Is a Word of *Inspiration*

Paul likens a Christian to a soldier, an athlete, and a farmer. These are occupations that require inspiration to push the individual through the drudgery of preparation. The soldier is inspired by victory in battle, so he prepares to fight the enemy. The athlete is inspired by the possibility of winning a medal, so he trains when he would rather rest. The farmer is inspired by the potential yield of the seeds he puts in the ground to feed himself and his family as well as keep others from hunger; so he plants in faith with no guarantee the crop will produce a harvest.

People today need inspiration too! We need hope from God to tell us we can do it when we are not sure. Believers are encouraged to walk with God, train for godliness, sow goodness, flee youthful lust, and run with endurance the race that is set before us. We cannot do this in our own power. We need inspiration and encouragement from the Bible.

The Passage Is a Word of *Motivation*

Inspiration is like a jolt of electricity that starts an engine. Motivation is more like the fuel providing internal drive to see the task completed. The truth of Philippians 4:13 can provide the motivation when we hit plateaus or seem to be going backward and feel like giving up. "I can do all things" is motivation to keep trusting and trying when tempted to give up.

The Passage Is a Word of *Consolation*

I saw a video testimony of a man who retired from his job and started a business. He invested a substantial portion of his life savings to fund his new venture. As business declined, he invested the rest of his retirement to keep it going. The business failed, and he went bankrupt. He was able to find a couple of other jobs, none of which worked out. He was a devout Christian; I am sure he believed God was leading him in his endeavors and claimed the promises of God along the way. Maybe he quoted Philippians 4:13 regularly.

His business still went under. We can speculate as to the cause. Maybe he misinterpreted the will of God in starting the business. Maybe he should have closed it earlier and salvaged what remained of his life savings. Or maybe God allowed him to start the business and allowed it to fail in order to show him that

God has the ability to get him through a worst-case scenario. It is a sad story in many ways, but there is one shining light. As it turns out, God gave the man the ability to endure great loss without losing his faith.

The simple meaning of Philippians 4:13 is that Paul had learned to deal with whatever circumstance he found himself in. Much or little, rich or poor, win or lose, in prison or out, he would get through by the power of Christ within him.

This verse is not a mantra that shields us from hard times. Nor is it a magic spell to force God to do what we want. It is a promise from God to carry us through the highs and lows of life.

NO SLAM DUNK

Have you ever wanted to experience the thrill of dunking a basketball in an NBA game? I have! Can you see yourself as Michael Jordan going airborne at the free-throw line and slamming it into the net? I can! The problem is I look more like a basketball than I look like Michael Jordan. I have about seven feet of "can do" jump for a ten-foot basketball rim. It's not part of the "all things" God has in store for me.

I'm going to imagine a conversation between myself and a friend with a build similar to mine who argues that this verse in Philippians is a promise from God that they can dunk a basketball. The conversation may go something like this:

Friend: "Are you saying that Christ will give me strength to dunk a basketball?"

Me: "You are 5'7" and weigh over 200 pounds. That's a lot of faith."

Friend: "But you said I can do all things through Christ who strengthens me."

Me: "I didn't say that; God did. Sometimes God uses means to perform a miracle. If you use a trampoline, maybe you can dunk a basketball."

Friend: "I can't jump on a trampoline because it aggravates my vertigo."

Me: "Maybe you can climb a ladder and dunk the ball."

Friend: "I have bad knees and can't climb a ladder with a basketball in my hand."

Me: "Okay, lower the goal from ten feet to five, and then you can dunk the ball with ease."

Friend: "But that would be cheating the process. God doesn't want me to cheat, does he?"

Me: "You are right! You can't dunk a basketball. It is not God's will for you to dunk a basketball. So learn to be content in *not* dunking a basketball!"

Friend: "Thank you."

CONCLUSION

Philippians 4:13 is a verse that can inspire us to believe that God has greater things in store for us. It can motivate us to take action toward our God-given goals and dreams. It can also console us when we endure life's hardships or come up short of the goal. It is not a "promise verse" declaring we can do anything we want. Our wants are usually self-centered and fall far short of the great things God wants for us. "I can do all things through Christ who strengthens me" is Paul's divinely inspired understanding that by God's power, the apostle could do far more than he thought possible. And so can we.

CAN DO; GO DO

- ◇ Inspiration: Pray and ask God to show you one thing he wants you to do. Use the verse as inspiration to get started.

- ◇ Motivation: What is one thing you have started but haven't completed? Use this verse as motivation to keep the dream alive and complete the task.

- ◇ Consolation: What is an area of hurt, loss, or setback? Pour out your heart to God and receive the comfort Christ gives us to endure.

CHAPTER 2

SOMETHING BETTER THAN SELF-HELP

Personal development is a part of the discipleship process of growing in sanctification through God's grace.

"My help comes from the Lord, the maker of heaven and earth."

PSALMS 121:2

"If I could help myself, I wouldn't need help in the first place."

According to *Research and Markets*, the motivation and self-help industry is an eleven-billion-dollar enterprise. Promoters sell books, CDs, DVDs, downloads, live streaming, website subscriptions, webinars, seminars, retreats, apps, and coaching products. They claim to have the secret to fulfillment, achievement, health, wealth, relationships, and self-awareness.[1] Some people view these methods as an elixir for life. Others think the offerings of this industry amount to little more than snake oil.

---

1 https://www.researchandmarkets.com/reports/4847127/the-us-market-for-self-improvement-products

SELF-HELP, OR GOD'S HELP?

We are likely all in favor of people bettering themselves. We believe children should have food, clothing, shelter, and access to a good education so they have every opportunity to succeed. As adults, we optimally continue to grow and mature in spirit, soul, and body. Our desire should be to do better, live better, and help the world be a better place. Author and entrepreneur Jim Rohn agreed when he said, "So the best gift you can give to others, really, is your ongoing personal development—getting better, getting stronger, becoming wiser."[2]

The challenge is not in a person's inclination to want to be better. Such a desire seems to be natural and God given. The pitfall is in thinking we can be better without the help of God and for reasons other than the glory of God.

I don't believe the Bible is a proponent of a "self-help" philosophy that focuses on the betterment of one's self for one's self, by one's self, from inside one's self, for one's own personal gain, and in one's own personal power. One self is too small a number to achieve true greatness. Such an attitude is self-centered, if not atheistic. To the contrary, Jesus asked a serious question to anyone who wants to improve themselves in the absence of God: "What shall it profit a man if he gain the whole world and lose his own soul?" (Mark 8:36). We need more than self-help. We need God's help!

Nor does the Bible espouse that self-help can make one right with God. We have all heard the expression "God helps those who help themselves." It sounds right, but the phrase is not in the Bible! Self-help is no help when it comes to making us right with God. Self-help will not cause us to be good enough to get to heaven. God helps those who can't help themselves—when they

---

2   https://www.jimrohn.com/self-improvement/

call on Jesus to save them!

SET APART FOR GOD: SO LONG, SELF

Sanctification: The Act and Process of Becoming More Like Jesus

Scripture teaches a higher principle than self-help: biblical sanctification. Sanctification is the *act* of the believer being set apart for the plan and purpose of God. The believer becomes like the furniture and fixtures of the Old Testament temple—created for God's purpose and whose primary use was to serve God.

Sanctification can be understood in two aspects. When a person trusts in Christ as Savior and Lord, they are sanctified—set apart for God. They have been drafted onto God's team and renewed for God's use. This is the first aspect of sanctification.

Second, sanctification is the lifelong process of becoming more like Jesus in every aspect of life. We have been sanctified in salvation. We are being sanctified through consecration. Just as a baby grows into adulthood, the believer is to "grow up in every way into him who is the head, into Christ" (Ephesians 4:15 ESV). As we grow in the faith, our desire matures and becomes the impetus to be better and get better for God's glory and as a testament to God's transforming power in our lives.

Christian discipleship is the means by which the process of sanctification takes place. A Christian disciple is a follower of Christ. Discipleship is the intentional process of maturing as a follower of Christ. It involves an internal transformation in beliefs, attitudes, and actions. No believer "arrives" as a perfect follower; rather, the believer matures to reflect the image of Christ in life and lifestyle.

Biblical Discipleship and Personal Development

Christian discipleship and personal development are not mutually exclusive. Personal development is a component of discipleship. God will be better honored in a believer's life when Christ-like attitudes and actions are the norm. The two practices should be thought of as "both-and" instead of "either-or" thinking.

Believers Are Called to Christian Discipleship

The Westminster Shorter Catechism states, "The chief end of man is to glorify God and enjoy him forever."[3] This means our greatest joy is found in a relationship with God. We give glory to God when we live virtuous and productive lives motivated out of love for him. The overarching life purpose of every Christian is to follow Christ in all things and live a life that reflects him in beliefs, attitudes, and actions. This is what it means to be "conformed to his [Christ's] image" (Romans 8:29, Philippians 3:14).

Conforming to the image of Christ includes embracing the fruit of the Spirit: love, joy, peace, kindness, patience, gentleness, faithfulness, and self-control (Galatians 5:22). It also includes loving obedience to the disciplines of prayer, Bible study, worship, fellowship, giving, and service. These God-produced character traits (and others) will cause the believer to shine as a light in a dark world. Sanctification is the process of allowing Christ, through the power of the Holy Spirit, to develop in the believer the character and skills needed to reach one's God-given potential. It is a life transformed by renewing the mind according to the will of God (Romans 12:2).

Believers Can Benefit from Personal-Development Tools

The tools of personal development can help a believer grow as

---

[3] https://www.shortercatechism.com/resources/wsc/wsc_001.html

an individual and as a contributor to the community. Attributes such as punctuality, time management, goal setting, service, integrity, hard work, likeability, calculated risk, resilience, personal appearance, skill development, and a desire to succeed are all compatible with the Christian experience. A biblical approach to discipleship that incorporates the tools of personal development is an application of practical sanctification.

TO GOD BE THE GLORY

All should be done for the glory of God, not personal aggrandizement. Exchanging sinful habits for godly habits is putting to death the "deeds of the flesh" and concern for the self (Colossians 3:5). Developing as a person involves exchanging lies for truth, laziness for industry, and envy for appreciation of others' accomplishments; foregoing self-centered pride for humility, lust for purity, hate for love, and fear for faith; giving instead of getting, worshipping God instead of wanting more for self, and serving instead of being served. In the pursuit of God and the good gifts he provides his children, we want to strive to honor him with a life well lived.

What sets apart a biblical view of personal development is the believer's motive: the believer wants to become better for the glory of God in order to provide a better testimony to the transforming power of God and be a stronger servant in building the kingdom of God.

The Bible tells us to "put off the old man, which belongs to your former manner of conduct and is corrupt by deceitful desires, and be renewed in the spirit of your minds, and to put on the new man, created after the likeness of God in true righteousness and holiness" (Ephesians 4:22–24). In order to put off the old man, we have to change the way we think and change the things we do that keep us from reaching our God-given potential through Christ. New habits, new disciplines, and newfound purpose come from a mind renewed by the power of God. He is sanctifying us!

The sewer line in our house backed up a few years ago. It was disgusting! Tree roots had grown into the pipe and stopped all forward progress. I thought I would save money by digging up the clogged line myself and getting my plumber friend to fix the blockage and replace the damaged pipe. I started digging. Grass gave way to dirt, which turned to mud, which turned to the remains of what my family and I had eaten over the last few weeks. By the time the repairs were made, my clothes and boots were coated in dirt and much worse. The plumber was unscathed. He got the job done without getting dirty. I changed my clothes and threw the dirty ones away. To me, the old clothes weren't worth keeping. I vowed never to repeat an ordeal like that. I could not wait to put on fresh, clean clothes.

The attitude Paul promotes in Philippians 4:13 is like putting on new "faith" clothes. "I can do all things through Christ who strengthens me" is a challenge to dream new dreams and work to achieve new goals through the strength of Christ. The verse is not meant to weigh down struggling believers with more guilt or fear of failure. It is meant to lift us up by the grace of God and a plan of action.

CONCLUSION

We need God's help in pursuing a meaningful life on earth. Believers can benefit from some of the tools of the self-help movement when the motive is to use them to become more like Christ in attitudes and actions. Personal development is a component of the discipleship process of practical sanctification.

CAN DO; GO DO

- ◊ What part do we play in personal development?
- ◊ What is God's activity in our personal development?
- ◊ What area of your life could benefit from personal-development tools and improve your testimony to a watching world?

CHAPTER 3
BLESSED BURGERS: THE DEFINITION OF AND DESIRE FOR SUCCESS

"Oh Lord save us! Oh Lord grant us success."

PSALMS 118:25

"I believed if I worked hard, the Good Lord would bless me with success."

BILL MASON

Success is defined in many ways and comes in many forms. The standard measure of success usually involves a lot of work, dedication, and time. However, anomalies do happen. I heard a story of how the richest man in his town was asked to give a talk to a school assembly on the reasons for his financial success. After being announced by the school principal, he stood at the podium and began to talk. His remarks were brief:

> When I was a young man, I looked for ways to make money. I worked a full-time job during the week and sold fruits and vegetables at the farmers market on the weekends. In the beginning, I saved five cents and bought an apple, which I sold for ten cents. I took the

ten cents and bought two apples, which I sold for twenty cents. This went on for a while until my uncle died and left me ten million dollars. That's when I stopped working for money, and money started working for me.

For those of us who did not inherit more money than we can spend, the tried and true is the surest path to success.

One question well-meaning people ask me is "Does God want me to be successful?" Such a question suggests that achievement is a sin or that success is completely contrary to God's will. My answer is "God will give you victory in the areas in which he wants you to succeed and may also allow you to experience setbacks and failures along the way to pursuing your God-given dreams." Instead of doubting God's will for us to succeed, it is better to believe God wants us to succeed *more* than we do! As Paul wrote to the Corinthians, "Eye has not seen, nor ear heard, neither have entered into the heart of man the things which God has prepared for them that love him" (1 Corinthians 2:9).

Another question I am asked in relation to success and Philippians 4:13 is "Does this verse guarantee that I will be successful in whatever endeavor I pursue?" My answer is "It depends on how you define success and what it is you want to pursue." First of all, if success means achieving what we want instead of what God wants for us, the answer is no. As Tim Kizziar is quoted as saying in Francis Chan's book *Crazy Love*, "Our greatest fear should not be of failure but of succeeding at things in life that don't really matter."[4]

Secondly, if success means prioritizing fame, fortune, health, wealth, power, and personal ambition over God, the answer is no. God is not opposed to these things if they are sought with the right motive, but placing the pursuit of "things" above

---

4 Francis Chan, *Crazy Love: Overwhelmed by a Relentless God* (Colorado Springs, CO: David C. Cook, 2008), 93.

God is certainly not included in God's definition of success. As clergyman George Truett said, "There is no failure in God's will, and no success outside of God's will."[5]

Thirdly, our desire to succeed should include the benefit of others. Evangelist D. L. Moody's words are prescient: "The measure of a man is not how many servants he has but how many men he serves."[6] When we use our success to serve others, we are not only succeeding but also creating a life of significance.

WHAT IS SUCCESS?

Different people define success in many different ways. Consider some of the following statements:

- ◇ Success is the accomplishment of a goal or purpose.

- ◇ "Success is going from failure to failure without any loss of enthusiasm."—Winston Churchill[7]

- ◇ "Success is falling seven times and standing up eight."—Japanese proverb[8]

- ◇ "The key is not to worry about being successful but to instead work toward being significant."—Wintley Phipps[9]

- ◇ "Success is really nothing more than the progressive realization of a worthy ideal."—Earl Nightingale.[10]

---

5 https://www.inspiringquotes.us/topic/6347-no-failure
6 https://moodycenter.org/the-quotable-moody-d-l-moody-quotes/
7 https://www.bereaninsights.org/quote/winston-churchill-quote
8 https://guidable.co/culture/5-common-japanese-proverbs-that-make-you-ponder
9 https://www.oprah.com/omagazine/what-oprah-knows-for-sure-about-finding-success
10 Earl Nightingale, *The Strangest Secret*, (Merchant Books Online, 2013)

- ◇ "Success comes from doing the best you can with what you have where you are."—Jamie Gilbert[11]

- ◇ "Success comes in a can: 'I can.'"—Wally "Famous" Amos[12]

- ◇ "Success is no accident. It is hard work, perseverance, learning, studying, sacrifice, and, most of all, love of what you are learning or learning to do."—Pele[13]

- ◇ "Success is the continuing achievement of becoming the person God wants you to be and accomplishing the goals God has helped you to set."—Charles Stanley[14]

- ◇ Success is walking in the will of God, according to the Word of God, as a follower of the Son of God.

All of the above definitions have some merit, but I would define success in this way:

Success is the process of growing as a follower of Christ while working toward our God-given dreams and goals and trusting him to accomplish them.

THE BIBLE AND SUCCESS

Does the Bible promote success? The Bible promotes God! He is the "Alpha and Omega." He is to be the first, the last, and

---

[11] Joshua Metcalf and Jamie Gilbert, *Burn Your Goals* (Morristown, NC: Lulu Publishing, 2015), 177.

[12] http://www.skatewhat.com/russhowell/WebPage-Quotes-FloatingMenu.

[13] https://laidlawscholars.network/posts/success-is-no-accident#:~:text=Pele

[14] Charles Stanley, *Success God's Way* (Nashville: Thomas Nelson, 2000) 3.

everything in between. Success without God is fool's gold; it looks real but is ultimately worthless. As Jesus told his disciples, "Seek first the kingdom of God, and his righteousness, and all these things shall be added to you" (Matthew 6:33).

When we put God first and walk with him, and implement his principles for living, we *are* a success! Seek God and success will follow. Consider some of the concepts of Christian success.

Success Is a By-product of Following God

After the death of Moses, God spoke to Joshua about successfully leading the people of Israel into the Promised Land. Moses told his apprentice Joshua: "This book of the law shall not depart from your mouth, but you shall meditate on it both day and night, that you may be careful to do all that is written in it. For then you will make your way profitable, and then you will have good *success*" (Joshua 1:8; emphasis added). Joshua accomplished the goal because he sought the Lord and brought the people into the Promised Land God's way.

Hundreds of years later, the elderly King David challenged his younger son and the future king Solomon to follow God fully and put him first: "And keep the charge of the Lord your God, to walk in his ways, in keeping his statutes, his commands, his rule and his testimonies, as it is written in the law of Moses, *that you may prosper* in all that you do and wherever you turn" (1 Kings 2:3 ESV; emphasis added). The word "prosper" can be understood as "success." As long as Solomon kept the charge of the Lord, he succeeded.

Jesus reinforced the teaching of putting God first during his earthly ministry. Two instances come to mind. The first occurred when Jesus was in the desert and tempted by the devil. Satan offered Jesus power and glory over all earthly kingdoms—the ultimate example of worldly success. Jesus replied to him, "Be gone, Satan! For it is written, 'You shall worship the Lord your

God, and him only shall you serve'" (Matthew 4:9–10 ESV). To pursue success ahead of God or to use God as a mere strategy to succeed is idolatry!

The second instance is expounded by Jesus in his teachings. Jesus challenged the crowds to not worry about what they would eat, drink, or wear but to "seek first the kingdom of God, and all these things will be added to you" (Matthew 6:33). Pursuing God first is success. Reaching our God-given goals and dreams are a by-product of following him.

Success Brings Contentment in the Pursuit of Achievement

I believe the apostle Paul would agree with my proposed definition of success as the process of growing as a follower of Christ while working toward our God-given dreams and goals and trusting him to accomplish them.

Paul wrote the book of Philippians from prison—certainly not a place we would naturally equate with success. Yet Paul understood that life is a process of setbacks and temporary defeats on the way to ultimate victory in Christ. His difficult circumstances did not determine his view of life or detrimentally affect his walk with God. He was a success because he followed Christ and did the will of God from the heart. His prison cell, where prisoners went to be punished and isolated, became a retreat from the distractions of daily life and a place to listen to God and write what he heard.

God's call for Paul was to pursue the mandate God had placed in his heart: to preach the gospel to the ends of the earth (Mark 16:15). So powerful was his vision that he was willing to endure hardship, alienation, persecution, imprisonment, poverty, and pain. Paul's answer to all that he experienced: "I have learned the secret of being content in every situation.... I can do all things through Christ who strengthens me."

Paul's ability to trust God for the results gave him contentment while striving for achievement. The two do not have to be contradictory.

Consider some current examples: A pastor will work hard to achieve church growth, yet he is content with the flock in his charge. A business wants to serve more people and make more sales, but the owner is content to provide great care for existing customers. An athlete wants to win every game but is content to train to do his or her best, whether they win or lose. Contentment is taking solace in God for our present circumstances while believing and working out the possibility of doing more.

WILL WE SEEK SUCCESS?

The question is not "Does God want me to succeed?" The question is "Will I step up and pursue the success God has for me?" To answer yes to the question requires seeking the will of God for our lives and taking responsibility to pursue it. It will take prayer and faith to believe we can do it in God's power. It takes action to work toward our goals and persevere until we reach them. It will require a "work of faith, labor of love, and endurance of hope in Jesus" (1 Thessalonians 1:3).

Several reasons come to mind as to why we should seek success.

We Will Grow as Disciples of Christ

The can-do mindset of Philippians 4:13, based on the foundation of Christ and his Word, needs to be developed in order to succeed. This mindset requires seeking God's will for our lives and prayerful dependence on him while we work to accomplish what we believe he wants us to do. Growing as a disciple requires guidance from the Holy Spirit when we are not convinced of what to do. This growth involves embracing and developing the disciplines of worship, fellowship in a local church, helping others, and service and witness in the community, to name a few.

We Can Use Success as a Platform to Honor God

In a world that values achievement and success, we need more Christians to be successful in their God-given crafts and vocation. We need more Christians of all walks of life to use their gifts and talents as a platform to speak out for God and show the tangible benefits of their faith. Proverbs assures all Christians, "Do you see a man skilled in his work? He shall stand before kings. He shall not stand in the presence of the unknown" (Proverbs 22:29).

In Super Bowl LII, the Philadelphia Eagles defeated the New England Patriots 41–33 to win their first NFL football championship. Eagles backup quarterback Nick Foles was named the Super Bowl MVP. He completed twenty-eight of forty-three passes for 373 yards and three touchdowns. He also caught a one-yard touchdown pass on a trick play known as the "Philly Special." The game was watched by over 103 million viewers worldwide.

In the post-game press conference, Foles was candid in who should get the glory: "I wouldn't be out here without God, without Jesus in my life. I can tell you that first and foremost."[15] His success on the football field and his willingness to speak about his faith brought honor to God, and Nick gained the respect of other players for his hard work and sincere faith.

Success Gives Us the Ability to Help Others

We are all called to serve God, give of our resources to help others, and spread the gospel. But we can't give what we don't

---

15 https://billygraham.org/story/super-bowl-mvp-nick-foles-i-wouldnt-be-here-without-jesus-in-my-life/

have! We are limited in what we can do for others when we are not able to do for ourselves. Success-minded people understand the joy of advancing in their God-given pursuits and helping others so that the people they help can have an opportunity to be successful too.

Bill Mason grew up poor in East Tennessee. His parents gave a lot of love to him and his four brothers and two sisters, but not much in the way of material goods. Bill had drive. He wanted to do well in life—not just for himself but also to help others. He worked hard at his job and moved up and down the East Coast when promotions came along. He often worked more than one job in order to get ahead.

Bill saw an opportunity to purchase a fast food franchise and took it. He and his family all worked in the business. They worked hard, managed the store well, and eventually were able to purchase other franchise stores. Bill believed in work but also understood God had been good to him. In return, Bill was generous to his church, the community, and his employees.

I was having lunch with Bill at one of his restaurants, and an employee approached us with a big smile on her face and asked if she could get us anything. We said we were fine, and she went to check on other tables. When she got out of hearing range, Bill told me a little story about the server.

"Did you see that person? She used to never smile. She was a good worker, but I kept her in the cooking area because she looked like she was mad all the time, and I did not want her to scare the customers," he said. "I found out why she didn't smile; she was missing a lot of teeth!"

He went on to tell me, "She could not afford to have her teeth worked on, so I went to a dentist friend and asked if he would give me a discount if I paid for her dental repairs. He agreed to do it, and now she smiles all the time!"

Bill never went to college, but he served on the board of a

local college. He did not have a background in finance but pulled together some local business people and started a community bank. He was not a good cook but purchased a fast-food franchise that made him financially independent. Throughout his life, he helped a lot of people in many different ways. His response: "I thank the good Lord for all he's done for me."

Our success should benefit others.

Our Success May Inspire Others to Achieve Greater Things

My wife, Carol, has taught high school English for years. She is a National Board–certified teacher and received "Teacher of the Year" at her school. She works hard at her craft of teaching high school students to become better readers, writers, and critical thinkers. She has taught hundreds. Many have gone on to complete college degrees. Some have received academic scholarships to elite schools. To this day, she receives word from some of her former students about the influence she had on their life. She sees her work as a calling from God. She is very successful at what she does and has instilled her educational success in others.

Success Is a Way to Maximize the Stewardship of the Life God Has Given Us

We are only on the planet for a short time. Yet what we do in this life matters forever. Chances are that anyone reading this book is living better than most people in the world! Take advantage of the opportunities God has given you. Don't waste your life by hiding your light under a basket. Seeking to be successful in life is a great way to shine for God and do good! Remember the words of British missionary C. T. Studd: "Only one life will soon be past. Only what's done for Christ will last."[16]

---

[16] https://www.epm.org/blog/2013/Jun/10/day-eternity

CONCLUSION

Success is the process of growing as a follower of Christ while working toward our God-given dreams and goals and trusting him to accomplish them. When we understand success as a by-product of pursuing God, we begin to see how God wants us to succeed. True success seeks to leave a legacy that will glorify God and benefit people.

CAN DO; GO DO

- Write one success goal you believe God wants you to pursue.
- What steps are you taking to successfully complete the goal?

CHAPTER 4
GOD'S LOVE IS BETTER THAN SELF-LOVE

Realizing how much God loves us is far greater than self-esteem.

"For no one ever hated his own body, but nourishes and cherishes it, just as the Lord does the church."

EPHESIANS 5:29

"God looks at you, and he loves you simply because he made you."

RICK WARREN

What do we see when we look in the mirror? Narcissus was the most handsome of young men. He was a child of deities from Greek mythology. Many fell in love with his attractive features. Their love, however, went unrequited because Narcissus could never love someone who was not as lovely as he.

While hunting in the woods, Narcissus was thirsty and found a pool of water from which to drink. He saw his reflection in the water and fell in love, mesmerized by his own good looks. He had finally found someone as beautiful as himself! But every time Narcissus went to kiss the image in the pond, it turned to ripples. Fixated with his own image but never able to touch it, Narcissus died of despair and thirst.

If Hollywood were to make a movie of the life of Narcissus, the final scene would show his distraught expression as he seeks to kiss himself for the last time, his head dropping into the water while soft little waves project away from his lifeless body. As the film fades to black, we would hear Carly Simon singing "You're So Vain" in the background

The story of Narcissus strikes an extreme chord with the self-centered "selfie" love so prevalent on popular social-media platforms.

HEALTHY AND UNHEALTHY SELF-ESTEEM

The self-esteem movement of the 1960s and '70s operated under the premise that if we made people feel better about themselves, they would be more psychologically adjusted and have the desire to do better in school, work, and life in general. So schools stopped using red markers to point out mistakes because it seemed too harsh. Students were given daily verbal doses of compliments, deserved or not. Recognizing students for hard work and achievement was switched to affirmation for mere participation. As a result, children's confidence in their abilities went up, while their testing scores went down.

In sports, children were given participation ribbons and trophies just for being on the team. Recreational soccer leagues stopped keeping score so the children on the losing team would not feel defeated. The obvious reality of winners and losers gave way to the mantra "Everyone's a winner!"

We should be quick to point out the slightest good in people, especially children. They have fragile egos and need to be built up physically, mentally, and spiritually. But seeking to boost their nascent self-esteem by saying everyone is great when it is clearly not the case is not healthy. Nor is it truthful.

Healthy Self-Esteem

The Mayo Clinic touts the attributes of healthy self-esteem: it can give more confidence, assertiveness, self-respect, and less concern for the negative perception of others.[17] People with healthy self-esteem are better able to form healthy relationships and are less likely to stay in unhealthy ones. They also tend to be more resilient and can "bounce back" from a setback.

On the other hand, those who struggle with low self-esteem are more prone to thoughts of unworthiness, discouragement, anxiety, and perceived weaknesses. They believe other people have greater skills, are more valued, and are more capable of success.

Healthy self-esteem is beneficial to the psyche, but there can be negative effects of unhealthy high self-esteem. According to Science Daily, individuals with an unhealthy high self-esteem are more likely to display defensiveness by blaming others and providing excuses when speaking about past transgressions or threatening experiences.[18]

The negative effects of unhealthy high self-esteem are reinforced by social psychologists David Dunning and Justin Kruger in a study conducted to evaluate how people view their social and intellectual abilities. Participants were tested in humor, English grammar, and logic. The study found that those testing in the very low twelfth percentile actually believed themselves to be in the sixty-second percentile. This finding, known as the

---

17   https://www.mayoclinic.org/healthy-lifestyle/adult-health/in-depth/self-esteem/art-20047976
18   https://www.sciencedaily.com/releases/2008/04/080428084235.htm

Dunning–Kruger effect, concludes that many people overestimate their abilities but lack the self-awareness to realize it.[19]

There is an opposite danger on the self-esteem spectrum: unhealthy low self-esteem. People in this category can struggle with guilt, shame, feelings of inadequacy, and inferiority. They can feel beat down by rejection, failure, bullying, and their own harsh inner critic. As a result, some see themselves as having little value, which can lead to poor moral choices, social withdrawal, diminished faith, and depression. People with unhealthy low self-esteem can also struggle to believe they are loved by God.

Such studies in psychology have verified what the Bible has revealed for thousands of years: we are prone to "think more highly of ourselves than we ought" (Romans 12:3). Pride, arrogance, vanity, lack of humility, disrespect, unkindness, and an inflated view of oneself are all evidence of the downward drag of sin.

ESTEEMED BY GOD

I think it is best to *not* think in terms of self-esteem. Why? Because our value and worth are not determined by how good or bad we feel about ourselves. Nor is it made real by what others think of us. The way we see ourselves should be determined by God. How does God see us?

We Are Special Creations of God

The Bible tells us that humans are made in the "image of God" and have special value and worth. We bear the likeness of our Creator. Though the image has been marred by sin, we still reflect his likeness in several ways. For example, we are

---

19   https://www.ncbi.nlm.nih.gov/pubmed/10626367

spiritual beings with souls that respond to God. We also have intelligence to create, reason, and engineer the most intricate of projects. We are relational and can distinguish our family lines for generations. We have a moral compass to know right and wrong and the self-awareness to ask "Why?" We are not God, nor will we become a god. But we have special value and worth because we bear his likeness.[20]

We Are Loved by God

In addition to being made in the image of God, we are loved by God and should see ourselves this way. We are loved not because of what we do but because of who God is: "God is love" (1 John 4:8). The greatest example of God's love for us is that he sent Jesus to die on the cross to save us from our sins. Think about this: Jesus died before we were born. Before we ever committed a sin, he had already paid for it: "For God so loved the world that he gave his only begotten Son, that whosoever would believe in him should not perish, but have everlasting life" (John 3:16).

We Are Made New by Christ

Because of what Christ has done for us, according to the Bible, we are children of God: accepted, adopted, renewed, redeemed, united with Christ, liberated, chosen, a holy priest, victorious, conquering, blood bought, Spirit transformed, born again, set apart, ambassador, light bearing, upward going, forgiven, clean, loved, grace receiving, saved, safe, secure, protected, precious, transformed, fruit producing, blessed, heir and joint heir with Christ. We are special possessions, blessed by the workmanship of God. We have been made new! We are not who we feel we are; we are who Christ says we are. Self-esteem is an inadequate substitute for discovering the deeper truth of who we are in Christ.

---

20 Rick Warren, *The Purpose Driven Life* (Grand Rapids, MI: Zondervan, 2002) 172.

God Has a Plan for Us

Life is more than an aimless struggle to survive. It is true that life has its difficulties and it is "through much tribulation [that] we inherit the kingdom of God" (Acts 14:22). Yet the apostle Paul was convinced that God would fulfill his plan for the believers at Philippi: "Being confident of this, that he who began a good work in you shall continue to complete it until the day of Christ Jesus" (Philippians 1:6).

I am convinced he will fulfill his plan for us all as we put into practice the principles gleaned from Philippians 4:13.

As a preacher, at the end of a sermon I would extend an invitation for anyone who wanted to leave their seat and meet with me at the altar. People would respond for an array of reasons: prayer, guidance, releasing of burdens, making public a commitment to Christ—all sorts of spiritual reasons.

On one occasion, a woman came forward. She had been attending the church for some time, and my wife and I had gotten to know her. As she approached me, she could hardly wait to get out the words: "Pastor Todd, I've been healed." I wasn't aware she had been sick! I was hesitant to ask what she had been healed from, but she added, "God has taken away some emotional scars." I found out later that she had been in an abusive marriage and had struggled with low self-esteem. On that day, God showed her she was infinitely more valuable than how she had been treated or how negatively she thought of herself. She realized she was esteemed by God!

CONCLUSION

How God sees us is so much greater than how we see ourselves. Thinking better of ourselves is okay but doesn't catch the wind of the Spirit and lift us out of nagging self-doubt.

Realizing who I am in Christ is infinitely more powerful than the self-generated belief, either positive or negative, of what I believe I am or can be. Our ultimate value and worth comes from being a child of God, not from status or ability.

CAN DO; GO DO

- ◊ Would you say your worth is based more in God's love for you or your own personal accomplishments?
- ◊ Reread the four reasons why you are esteemed by God and thank him for his love.

SECTION 2

"I"

To reach our God-given potential, we must take responsibility for doing our part to pursue it.

*"**I** can do all things through Christ who strengthens me."*

CHAPTER 5
FAT-INIZATION

Responsibility is the right choice. Any other is a poor choice.

"So then each of us will give an account of himself to God."

ROMANS 14:12

"If you really want to do something, you'll find a way. If you don't, you'll find an excuse."

JIM ROHN

I had been overweight for years. A pound or two or three a year over two decades will add up. To misquote a phrase, a little leaven had turned me into a lump.

My calling was somewhat of a sedentary lifestyle. I pastored churches for twenty-two years. A lot of time as a pastor is spent praying, preparing messages, attending meetings, and ministering to people. It is a very rewarding life but does not naturally lend itself to calorie burning. The result was my "fat-inization."

In addition, it seemed as if every time I went to church, there was food: coffee and donuts at men's morning Bible study; chips and cookies at committee meetings; dinner before Wednesday-night services. When I visited church members in their homes, we would usually have some dessert.

I was fifty pounds (maybe more) overweight. I knew I needed to lose weight but kept putting it off instead of taking it off.

I rationalized and made excuses for my obesity. My inner sound bites sounded something like "I look better than most of my preacher friends." "My metabolism has slowed," "Parishioners like plump preachers." "I can lose weight any time I want." My excuses were justification for extra trips to the refrigerator and to the rack for larger men at the clothing store.

Over time, I became discouraged and engaged in self-pity. I did not want to be fifty pounds overweight but couldn't seem to lose it. I would go through periods of serious dieting and drop a few pounds, only to put it back on, and a little more. I started exercising, believing if I just walked a little on a treadmill, I would get to my ideal weight. The problem was not the treadmill. The problem was that I did not make a habit of exercising regularly, and I kept eating more calories than I was burning. The discouragement did not come from lack of a plan. I failed to be responsible in executing the plan.

Then, I convinced myself I was a victim. Many of the pastors I knew were as large, or larger, than I. We were in a "calling full of calories" and had no choice but to partake. After all, we would not want to offend our parishioners by snubbing their hospitality.

And my waistline kept expanding.

Then I started to play the blame game. I told myself it was the secretaries' fault for having candy in the office; the church's fault for expecting me to eat at Wednesday-night dinners and all church fellowships; a church member's fault for offering dessert when I visited them. Though none of them ever forced me to eat anything or criticized me when I politely declined their culinary delicacies (which was not very often), I still held them responsible for my obesity. If it wasn't for them, I would have a physique like Jesus.

Rationalizing, being discouraged, playing the victim, blaming others—none of that helped me lose weight. My clothes were getting tighter, and the scales were going higher. I remember telling my wife, "I either have to lose weight or get a new wardrobe."

That was a few years ago. Now I am forty pounds lighter and working on taking off the rest. What made the difference? It all started when I took complete responsibility for my weight! Once that was set in my mind, I could take the next steps to health and wellness.

I took ownership of my physical condition, and my health and eating began to improve. I started eating more veggies and fewer sweets and formed the habit of going to the gym. I prayed diligently for God's grace to lose the pounds. I confessed that I was a food addict and needed his help. I got an accountability partner to encourage me in my weight-loss goals.

I still struggle with weight, but I am nowhere near what I used to weigh. I was able to overcome, and so can you! It all started when I took responsibility for my situation.

A DEFINITION OF "RESPONSIBLE"

We can define responsible in the following way: being accountable for our actions; taking ownership of the condition of our life or situation, with the intent of making it right, and not blaming others or making excuses for our poor choices and lack of progress and success.

At the heart of responsibility is the belief that God loves us so much that he will call us to account for our actions.

PITFALLS OF RESPONSIBILITY

Pitfalls are flimsily camouflaged pits that unwitting prey fall into. The term has come to refer to hidden problems or unrecognized dangers. Not taking responsibility is a pitfall. Let's look at some of the most obvious pitfalls of irresponsibility.

Denying There Is a Problem

It was not until I was medically categorized as obese that I admitted I had a weight problem. Before then, I would look in the mirror and think, *I looked pretty good.*

Denial can play games with our heads. We might admit a problem exists but deny it is our responsibility. Sometimes we are like little children who have spilled juice on the carpet. When asked who spilled the juice, we say, with juice box in hand, "I don't know. It wasn't me." We have to stop denying there is a problem and take responsibility.

Delaying Taking Action

"I'll do something about it someday." "I'll get my life together someday." "I'll get out of debt someday." "I'll go on a diet someday." "I'll mend the relationship someday." Business consultant Brian Tracey calls this living on "Someday I'll." The only way to get off this overcrowded desert island is to take responsibility. Stop hesitating! The longer we wait, the longer it takes. Procrastination is the assassination of growth. Stop killing your progress!

Why do we delay? Perhaps we are too lazy to do something about it. Responsibility takes energy and hard work—physical, mental, emotional, relational, and spiritual work. When we are lazy in our responsibilities, we must remember what Jesus said: "To whom much is given, much will be required" (Luke 12:48). Repent of laziness, and walk in God's power!

Justifying Irresponsible Actions

We miss deadlines, don't reach our weight-loss goals, don't follow a budget, or cheat on a test. When asked about it, we get defensive and try to justify our actions. We may say we have a special reason that makes us an exception to the rule. We may argue that what we were tasked with doing was an unreasonable expectation. Or we may say, "In comparison to so-and-so, I am doing just fine." None of the reasons make the outcome right.

Take responsibility for things that are in your control.

Blaming Others

Some people believe the only responsibility they should take for failure is to find someone else to blame. They believe that if something goes wrong with their life, it is because of someone else. Blame is not the answer. It doesn't solve the problem or get us out of the predicament. A situation may be the fault of someone else, but it is our responsibility to fix it and move forward.

If others have failed or wronged us, we can hold them accountable, but we should not project responsibility onto them. It is lame to cast blame!

Be the bigger person and stop the blame game:

- ◇ The fast-food restaurant is not responsible for our weighing too much.
- ◇ Mommy and Daddy are not responsible for our poor adult choices.
- ◇ Teachers are not responsible for our poor study habits.
- ◇ The church is not responsible for our lack of love for God.
- ◇ The preacher is not responsible for our not knowing the Bible.

- ◇ The credit card companies are not responsible for our spending too much.
- ◇ The world does not owe us a living.
- ◇ God is not to blame for our lack of progress.
- ◇ Other people are not responsible for our poor attitude.
- ◇ Our job is not to blame for our dissatisfaction with life.

Don't point the finger at someone or something else. For every finger we point toward someone, there are three pointing back at us. Point the finger in the direction of the one who can make a difference: yourself. "Thou shalt take aim and blame" is not one of the Ten Commandments.

Wallowing in Self-Pity/Pouting and Moping

According to Lifescience contributor Stephanie Pappas, pigs wallow in mud for various reasons: to cool down body temperature, remove parasites, mark their territory, and possibly because they just like to![21] Could it be that one reason why people wallow in self-pity is because we like to?

I have heard a saying that a director used on the set of a hit TV show: "If you pout, you're out." It supposedly dramatically cut down the whining during production. Self-pity is not the answer. No one wants to come to our pity party. We have to stop feeling sorry for ourselves and take responsibility for our lives.

Self-pity can lead to self-loathing. We can begin to hate ourselves for our deficiencies rather than help ourselves by taking responsibility. Despair can lead to depression. It is a downward trend with no upside. God gives us dignity, value, and worth.

Look up, stand up, and ratchet up the responsibility.

---

21   https://www.livescience.com/13953-pigs-evolved-mud-wallowing.html

Playing the Victim

I was at a stoplight one night when a drunk driver struck the car behind me. The force was so hard that the car behind me was catapulted into the rear of my car, totaling both vehicles. The elderly couple in the other totaled car had to go to the hospital. Thankfully, they were not seriously injured. I was not injured, but my car was crushed. The police arrested the inebriated driver and took him to jail.

My car was not new, but it was paid for and ran well. When the insurance told me what they would give me as a settlement, I felt doubly victimized. What they were offering would not pay for a new car, or even what I would consider reliable transportation!

It angered me to think that while driving home, minding my own business, obeying the law, someone who was reckless and driving under the influence of alcohol had upended my life. My vehicle was totaled, and I had to take out a loan to purchase reliable transportation. That is not right!

But I could not change what happened. I had to let it go and get another vehicle. We cannot always control what happens to us, but we can control how we respond to being victimized.

(What If I Have Been the Victim?)

We may have been a victim, but we don't have to play the victim. Maybe we could not control what happened to us, but we can control how we respond. It can be hard, and some traumatic experiences take longer to heal than others. Some may involve the need for professional counseling. At some point, sooner being better than later, we have to take responsibility to move on with our lives. It may take time to completely heal from the damage of being victimized, but by God's grace, we can do it.

One way to move on from a traumatic event is to ask, "What happens now? How can I take responsibility to move beyond?"

For instance, if someone has committed a crime against us, we can seek justice. Assailants should not be allowed to go unchallenged. If we turn them in to the police, it may prevent the one who did wrong from doing it again. It can also help bring closure to a huge injustice. Prayer and talking with trusted friends can help us process how to move on.

Moving on should leave space for forgiveness. Forgiving is not forgetting. Traumatic experiences are not erased from memory—nor is forgiving ignoring what happened to us. That is denial. Forgiveness is the choice to accept what has happened to us and to let go of the desire to retaliate or seek revenge. It is the choice not to let what happened to us keep us from moving forward. Forgiveness releases us from the soul-wrenching baggage of hate and malice toward someone. Complete forgiveness may take a long time, but it has to begin somewhere. If we take responsibility to become forgiving people, God will honor our faith.

A clarification: If someone has committed a crime against us, it is not our fault. We did not deserve it. No one deserves to be raped, robbed, molested, abused, assaulted, libeled, or slandered. Such evil is the sad result of living in a sin-cursed world.

But we must take responsibility to overcome it. Do we need to bring the perpetrators to justice? Do we need to get counseling to help with the trauma? Do we need to put boundaries in place to prevent the likelihood of it happening again? Do we need to start a movement that will prevent it from happening to others? We can move beyond the trauma with God's help and our resolve to take responsibility to overcome.

Making Excuses

Don't make excuses! Make promises to yourself and find a way to keep them. Every excuse we make can be met with a responsible response:

- ⋄ "I was late because I was stuck in traffic." Take responsibility to leave earlier and get there early.

- ⋄ "I can't lose weight because I have low metabolism." Exercise more, eat healthier, and stop eating too much of the wrong foods. Get an accountability partner to keep on track.

- ⋄ "I tried to get out of debt, but I don't make enough." Make more; spend less. Live below your means. Get on a budget and stick to it.

Every excuse we make is a step away from the light of freedom and a downward step into the pitfall of defeat.

Excuses sabotage our inner desire to truly be responsible. Excuses are boa constrictors that choke the life out of responsibility and eat accomplishment as prey. Many people will make excuses instead of taking responsibility. We are better than that!

Adopt the expression "If it's meant to be, it's up to me." Own it, and success will own you.

Letting the Fear of Failing Keep Us from Trying

Taking responsibility for our lives can be a scary thing. There is no safety net of excuses to fall on. If we try and don't succeed, we may experience loss. If we fail, there is no one to blame. Fear of failure causes inertia and keeps us from taking action. We must use responsibility like a rocket to launch upward and get our life to soar.

Here are four thoughts to liberate a life against the fear of failure:

- ⋄ Everyone fails before they succeed.

- ⋄ Failing doesn't make us a failure. We just figured out a way it doesn't work.

◊ If we face our fears and try, we may eventually succeed.

◊ God still loves us whatever the outcome.

Steve Jobs didn't invent the iPhone on the first try. Thomas Edison tried hundreds of times before inventing a light bulb that worked. We enjoy a high quality of life today because willing people took great responsibility for their failings and kept trying until they found a way to make it work.

Be one of the great ones!

Thinking Responsibility Is Too Hard or Overwhelming

How does one eat an elephant? One bite at a time.

We will see in another chapter that nothing is too hard with God's help. Nothing is overwhelming when we believe we are an overcomer. Rather than thinking about how hard a given task will be, remember the caliber of person you will become by taking responsibility. Losing forty pounds seemed too hard and overwhelming for me, but losing one pound forty times was doable.

You can do it!

Complaining to Others about How Unfair It Is

Complaining is not a solution-oriented way of communicating with ourselves. Dale Carnegie's first principle in his blockbuster business book *How to Win Friends and Influence People* is "Don't criticize, condemn or complain." Responsible people accept that life is hard and walking the path is demanding at times.

Find a shoulder to cry on every now and then, but don't wallow in the lap of the negative habit of complaining. Take responsibility for what you say to yourself and what you say to others.

Envying the Successful

Some people believe there is only so much success to go around, so if they have less, it is because someone else unfairly has more. Not so. Responsible people believe anyone can be successful if they trust in God, love others, work hard, and become great at what they do. Making someone smaller doesn't make us bigger.

Don't resent someone else's life. Become responsible for yours.

Substituting Lesser Things Instead of Doing the Responsible Thing

It was Saturday afternoon, and I had not finished my Sunday sermon. Actually, I had barely started my Sunday sermon. I did not feel like preparing a message, so I cleaned the garage. Though I was the only teaching pastor of the church and it was my responsibility to prepare and preach well, I wasn't feeling it. By the time I got into the mindset of preparation, I was physically tired and had run out of steam. I should have taken responsibility for the sermon long before Saturday night, but lesser things got in the way.

Needless to say, the message tanked. It was so bad that I didn't even want to hear it. I would venture to say that not even my mother cares much for a Sunday-morning sermon born out of a week's worth of my prioritizing other things that don't matter. Prioritizing "lesser things" is a pitfall to taking responsibility for the main thing. "First things first" is a responsible maxim for success.

Making More Poor Choices

In dealing with the public and working as a pastor for many years, I have noticed a spiritual condition that afflicts people. When someone refuses to take responsibility for their actions, they generally continue to make poor choices and in fact make poorer choices. In one instance, I tried to help a parishioner who became addicted to drugs. He knew it was wrong and said he wanted help. However, he would not go to rehab, never showed up for counseling, and would not go to meetings. His desire to get high turned into a need to get high.

To feed his addiction, he stole a gun from a relative and robbed a convenience store. He got caught and went to prison. Failure to take responsibility led to making poor, then poorer, choices and accelerated the downward momentum of self-sabotage. Author Dennis Waitley said, "A sign of wisdom and maturity is when you come to terms with the realization that your decisions cause your rewards and consequences. You are responsible for your life, and your ultimate success depends on the choices you make."[22]

Quitting

Perhaps the most regrettable consequence of not taking responsibility is that we quit and give up. Our irresponsible internal voice says, "I'll never get ahead" or "The system is rigged against me." Don't quit! Remember: the reason you are taking responsibility for your actions is to make your life better.

When our children were school age, my wife and I would take trips to Tennessee to see "Nana," their grandmother. On one of our visits, I drove by an auto repair shop and noticed an old 1962 Lincoln Continental. It had baby-blue paint, suicide doors, and was a mile long. I went inside the shop and asked if the owner was interested in selling the car. The shop manager said the car had some motor issues and repairs would be completed when the car owner paid him. I made an offer to purchase the car and asked the mechanic to speak to the owner. He said he would.

At the end of the week, I went back to the shop, excited about

---

[22] https://harveymackay.com/be-responsible-for-yourself/

the possibility of owning a classic car. Sadly, the owner was not interested in selling, and I had to say "bye-bye" to owning Big Baby Blue. We returned a year later, and the car was still in the garage lot, only now the air in the tires was lower and some rust was visible. It was still salvageable but needed more work. I asked again about the owner's willingness to sell the vehicle and received the same answer.

This went on for three years! Each time I went back, the car looked a lot worse, and my price went down. Finally, I decided I could not afford to restore the car. The owner's unwillingness to take responsibility for the upkeep of a beautiful vehicle made the value of the car almost worthless.

Your life is much more valuable than an old car. Cherish it as God does.

CONCLUSION

When I took responsibility for my physical condition, I became healthier. It wasn't easy, but it was the right thing to do. Not taking responsibility makes one's condition worse. Jesus said we will give an account on judgment day for what we say and do (Matthew 12:36). We can avoid responsibility, but we cannot avoid the consequences.

Give yourself afresh to God, and take responsibility for your actions.

CAN DO; GO DO

Look back over the pitfalls of responsibility I have listed for why we fail to take responsibility. Which two or three do you struggle with the most? Why?

CHAPTER 6
DATIVE CASE

We are responsible to God, ourselves, and others.

"Could it be that you have come to your royal position for such a time as this."

ESTHER 4:14

"If you can't get a miracle, become one."

NICK VUJICIK

As an English teacher, my wife knows all about grammar, sentence structure, syntax, and parts of speech. I, on the other hand, would rather make puns: "My wife teaches English; she has a lot of comma sense."

However, in school I learned about the dative clause in an English sentence. It is the indirect object of a sentence and usually preceded by the preposition "to" or "for"—thus the title of this chapter.

Who are we responsible *to*? What are we responsible *for*? I would say there are at least four areas of responsibility, and many others involving people and projects we are responsible for. The primary areas of responsibility: God, self, community (which would include family, church, work, neighborhood, school, country, and other organizations in which we choose to participate), and other people and situations where circumstances require us to get involved. There may be more, but I think there are no fewer than these.

We Are Responsible to God.

As it says in Romans 4:12, "So then each of us will give an account of himself to God." We are responsible for how we respond to God. Have you made a definite decision to trust Christ as your Lord and Savior? "I can do all things" can only be achieved *through* Christ! He is our source of hope, strength, and salvation. His sacrifice on the cross and resurrection from the dead was for the purpose of restoring us to a right relationship with God. He has done all of the work to provide salvation. It is our responsibility to trust and follow him.

It is also our responsibility to God to grow in our faith. The apostle Peter instructs Christians to "grow up" in our salvation (1 Peter 2:1–3). As such, we should ask spiritually grown-up questions like "Do I spend time in prayer and study of the Scripture? Am I generous in giving to God? Do I show true devotion and obedience to God? Am I living right by him? Am I treating other people the way I wish to be treated? Do I show proper love and reverence in worship?" We are responsible to God for being intentional in our Christian development.

We Are Responsible for Ourselves

It is our responsibility to make the most of the opportunities God provides. We must take responsibility for our physical, mental (thoughts), emotional (feelings), verbal (words), financial, relational, intellectual, vocational, and spiritual condition. It is to our advantage to hold ourselves accountable for our attitudes and actions.

Have you ever blamed parents, siblings, relatives, friends, enemies, coworkers, bosses, teachers, neighbors, strangers, your spouse, someone else's spouse, authorities, religious leaders, preachers, teammates, coaches, customers, clients, lawyers, doctors, businesses, banks, tools, equipment, the economy, jobs, the government, the weather, school, political parties, the fine print, the world (if I left out any, please insert)? They may have contributed to the situation, but if we continue to think they control our destiny, we have not taken responsibility.

For each person who has blamed obstacles and made excuses in their "less-than" life, there are others who hurdled over the obstacles and made a life worth living.

Nick Vujicic was born without arms or legs due to a rare medical condition known as phocomelia. As a child, he was bullied in school and suffered bouts of depression to the point of being suicidal. But as a teenager, Vujicik realized that being born without arms and legs was not a punishment from God. Instead, God could use his disability to inspire and encourage others going through hard experiences.

Now in his thirties, Vujicik is an international speaker, best-selling author, and has appeared on television and in movies. He is the CEO of the nonprofit ministry Life Without Limbs. He is also married to a woman named Kanae, and together they have four children. Nick has said, "If God can use a man without arms and legs to be His hands and feet, then He will certainly use any willing heart!"[23]

Take responsibility for yourself. God has great things in store for you!

We Are Responsible to Our Community

We were not made to live in isolation. We are called to live in fellowship with other believers and in the community God has placed us. The key questions to ask are "Am I contributing

---

23   christiantoday.com.au/news/nick-vujicic-man-without-limbs-shares-the-bible-verse-that-gave-him-purpose.html

to my community? Am I doing my part to make it better?"

A friend of mine who works for the government told me how he grew tired of bureaucratic meetings, which lasted too long and often devolved into little more than tense blame games. Public servants were reduced to accusing each other of creating their work problems. Needless to say, this led to poor morale and lack of communication in the office. My friend asked himself, *How can I make these meetings more peaceful?* He began to pray before meetings that God would give guidance to the conversations and help with the decisions, as well as making the meetings more peaceful. He immediately noticed that the environment became less tense; people began to offer solutions instead of complaints.

If we are a part of something, it is our responsibility to do our part to help make it better! God may have strategically placed us where we are "for such a time as this" (Esther 4:14).

Esther is an example from the Bible of someone who took responsibility for her community when it could have cost her life. She was a young Jewish woman being raised by her cousin Mordecai in the city of Suza. She was described as "having a beautiful figure and [being] lovely to look at" (Esther 2:7 ESV).

At the time, Xerxes was king of Persia and ruler over that region of the world. His queen, Vashti, fell out of favor with the king and was deposed. He decreed that women from all over the kingdom should be gathered up so that he might find a potential replacement. Esther was one of those women taken into the palace and prepared for an audience with the king. When Xerxes saw Esther, he was smitten! He set the royal crown on her head and made her queen—all without learning that she was a Jew.

While Esther was in the palace, Mordecai would sit in the king's gate, where people gathered to share news and hot gossip. It was there he heard of a plot to assassinate the king. He informed Queen Esther, who notified King Xerxes. The plot was foiled, and the perpetrators were hanged. Esther and her uncle saved the king.

Long after this incident, Xerxes promoted one of his officials, Haman the Agagite, to a position above all of the other officials. The king went so far as to decree that people must bow down and pay homage to Haman. Mordecai refused to comply because he believed it would be offensive to God. Haman instigated a plot to kill Mordecai and all the other Jews of the kingdom; he was even able to convince the king to pass another decree to annihilate all the Jews in one day!

Mordecai was distraught and Esther deeply disturbed. The Jews mourned their impending demise. All seemed hopeless. Mordecai asked Esther to go to the king and beg and plead with him to rescind his order. But Esther had not been summoned by the king in many days, suggesting she had fallen into disfavor. The law of the land declared that anyone who entered the king's presence unannounced was to be killed immediately. Yet if she did not go to the king, her cousin Mordecai and all of her people would be murdered. Esther had a dilemma. Did she let things continue on as they were, or did she take responsibility to speak to the king on behalf of her cousin and her people?

Esther went to the king, and his pleasure at seeing her saved her life: the king reached out his scepter to her. She then set up a situation whereby the intentions of Haman were exposed. The king was infuriated at Haman. Instead of Mordecai and the Jews being slaughtered, Haman was hanged. Mordecai was promoted to Haman's position, and the Jews were spared.

God had strategically positioned Esther in a place of responsibility in order to use her to protect her community, and she did so by taking responsibility.

We Are Responsible for Offering Our Help

Scripture says, "Whoever knows to do good and does not do it, to him it is sin" (James 4:17). The responsibility to offer our help is what Jesus referred to as "neighbor love," and he explained what he meant in the story of the Good Samaritan. Do you remember the story?

A traveler was going from the city of Jerusalem to Jericho when he was accosted by robbers who stripped him, beat him, and left him half dead. A priest came down the road but, when he saw the man, passed by on the other side. Next, a Levite came and purposefully ignored the victim. He passed by on the other side of the road as well. Finally, a Samaritan saw the man and went to him, bound up his wounds, and cleaned the cuts. He placed him on a donkey and took the wounded man to a hotel to rest and heal. The Samaritan also made arrangements to pay for the assaulted man's lodgings. The Samaritan did not know the traveler, and Samaritans and Jews largely hated one another; yet he made it his responsibility to do the traveler good.

God will bring people and situations into our lives as opportunities to take responsibility. This responsibility could be the need to lend a hand or help someone get back on their feet. Saying yes will bring success.

CONCLUSION

Taking responsibility for our lives is like moving from the back seat of the car to the driver's seat. No longer merely along for the ride, we are mapping the direction of the journey God has for us. The road will be bumpy and have turns and detours, but we will enjoy the thrill of what lies over the next hill.

Imagine how much better the world would be if people took seriously their responsibility to God, themselves, their community, and others.

Be the change you want to see!

CAN DO; GO DO

- ◊ In what area of responsibility would you say you struggle the most (God, yourself, community, people, or situations of need)? Why would you say this is so?

- ◊ Commit to being more responsible in at least one area relating to God (prayer, worship, giving, serving, Bible engagement).

- ◊ What is one area of need in your community (family, church, school, work, neighborhood, state, country), and how will you be responsible to help?

CHAPTER 7
CHOOSE YOUR HARD

Taking responsibility has many positive benefits but is not easy. Not taking responsibility seems to be the easy way out but brings hard consequences.

"For the moment all discipline seems painful rather than pleasant, but later it yields the peaceful fruit of righteousness to those who have been trained by it."

HEBREWS 11:12

"Once people stop making excuses, stop blaming others and take ownership of everything in their lives, they are compelled to take action to solve their problems."

JOCKO WILLINK

Motivational expert Brian Tracey said, "Accepting responsibility is one of the hardest of all disciplines, but without it, no success is possible."[24] Accepting responsibility for my weight forced me to do something I did not like: exercise. It also forced me not to do something I really liked: eat. Accepting responsibility is hard. It forces us to make changes to our

---

24 Brian Tracy, *No Excuses* (New York: MJF Books, 2010), 50.

lifestyles in order to make things right.

Not taking responsibility is hard as well! It can lead to regret and loss of self-respect and leave us wondering what might have been if we had been willing to take responsibility. Sometimes it comes down to "choosing our hard."

THE BENEFITS OF RESPONSIBILITY

The benefits of taking responsibility far outweigh the cost. Consider the following benefits as we say yes to taking responsibility for our lives.

It Helps Us Do God's Will and Understand Him Better

Jesus told a story of two brothers who were asked by their father to go into the vineyard and work (Matthew 21:29–31).

The first one said no but later changed his mind and went.

The second one said, "I will go," but never did.

Jesus asked his disciples, "Which son did the will of the father?"

The disciples replied, "The first."

What is the difference between the two brothers? They had the same father and shared the same DNA. Presumably they grew up in the same house. The difference is one took responsibility and the other did not. As a result of taking responsibility, the reluctant son accomplished the will of God.

Jesus said, "He who has my commands and keeps them is the one who loves me. And the one that loves me shall be loved by my Father, and I will love him, and *reveal* myself to him" (John 14:21; emphasis added). If you would like to do God's will and know him better, become a person of responsibility toward Jesus and life!

Our Faith Will Grow

My father had huge forearms like Popeye the sailor. Dad grew up on a farm and worked at a lumber mill in his youth. Eight hours a day, five days a week, he lifted heavy wooden boards with his hands and arms. The constant exercising of his muscles gave him great strength.

Faith is like a muscle: the more it's used, the stronger it gets. When we take responsibility for our lives, we begin to realize how much we need faith in God to see our dreams become reality. I will have more to say about the necessity of faith in the "Can" section.

We Will Have Power to Change

I am asked sometimes to consult with churches that have been in decline for years. When they seek advice, I try to be as thorough as I can in determining their strengths and areas needing growth. I look back over the history of the particular church, both the glory days and the lean years. I do a ten-year analysis of attendance, membership, baptisms, financial offerings, and surrounding community. I collate the data and then bring in the leadership for what I call a "current reality" workshop. In this meeting, we discuss how a loss of momentum and lack of change has brought them to their present condition. I then encourage them to take responsibility for their current reality and begin working at ways to change for the better. Churches that own their situations and take responsibility to make changes become healthier.

One church had been in decline for decades, and many of the members had lost hope in the future. Attendance had dwindled by half, and their budget could not support all of the paid staff and ministries. They did not see a way out but knew they had to do something or else close the church.

Change was painful. They had to let go of some personnel

positions and reduce the budget. Thankfully, God gave them the power to do it. Now attendance is stable, and church members have stepped up to do the work that staff were being paid to do. The spirit of the church is much better, and they have a sense of momentum. Taking responsibility for their situation gave them power to change.

I believe God has given people an innate desire to be better and do better—to reach our God-given potential in Christ. Sadly, sin has dulled the senses. The potential is there but needs revitalizing. Taking responsibility for ourselves and our situation is like cleaning silver dishes. As the polish is applied, the tarnish is wiped away, and the luster of the precious metal begins to shine.

Taking responsibility should create a desire to change into the shining vessel we were each made to be—one that brings glory to God. One of the greatest abilities is response-ability! Nothing changes until we take charge of our lives.

We Will See Positive Results

There is a tendency to think that taking responsibility is too painful. Just the opposite is true. Taking responsibility gives us the motivation to ramp up our game and get winning results.

Dan Cathy is the CEO of Chick-fil-A and successor to his father, Truett Cathy. Dan told the story of how a number of years ago, the home office would send mystery shoppers to the stores and give feedback on their experience at the restaurant.[25] The shoppers were asked to fill out a survey, and the last question asked was "Based on your experience, would you return to a Chick-fil-A?" Shockingly, 25 percent said no. A host of reasons were given by respondents: surly service, cold waffle fries, and dirty bathrooms, to name a few.

Cathy looked for someone to blame. He originally blamed the owner-operators for the problem, thinking they needed to

---

25 Dan Cathy, *The Problem in the Mirror; Rightnow media.*

spend more time in their restaurants. If the operators weren't to blame, then it was the home office staff or field operations staff. For two years, he beat up on other folks; they needed to get their act together so they could move the customer-satisfaction needle. But the needle never moved.

Mysteriously, someone left a book on Cathy's desk by Philip Crosby: *Quality Is Free*. In the book, Crosby suggests that business is a reflection of leadership. Cathy was confronted with the fact that he might be the source of the problem. He realized that if he took responsibility and changed and treated people better, it might affect the way Chick-fil-A stores treated their customers. Cathy became a student of quality—how to measure it and how to develop a culture of quality through personal execution.

Over time, the needle began to move. This only happened when Cathy realized there was a problem and that he had to look in the mirror for the solution. He took responsibility for the way he was affecting the quality of the stores and took responsibility to change himself and fix the problem. Today, Chick-fil-A sets the standard for fast-food customer satisfaction.

Our Reputations as People of Integrity Will Increase

People who take responsibility earn respect and build reputations of honesty and integrity. Responsible people admit when they have failed or done wrong, and they do all they can to make it right—not because they necessarily want to but because they value their reputation. They know that the short-term pain of telling the truth and doing the right thing will build long-term respect and the pleasure of a good reputation. King Solomon said, "A good name is to be chosen over great riches, and favor is better than silver or gold" (Proverbs 22:1). A favorable reputation is priceless.

SEAL commander Jocko Willink was leading a team of American and friendly Iraqi soldiers in Ramadi, Iraq, when a brutal firefight broke out. Amid the mayhem, men were screaming, bleeding, and dying. Sadly, it was a fight not against the enemy but against friendly forces. By the end of the confusing clash, one friendly Iraqi soldier was dead, and several of Willink's men were wounded. According to Willink, "It was only through a miracle that no one else was killed."[26]

Arriving back at base, he was immediately called to debrief the commanding officer about what had happened and what went wrong. Willink knew somebody would be held responsible. As he prepared his report, he detailed every mistake: every failure of planning, preparation, and execution of the operation. He also pointed out whom he believed should be blamed for the failure.

Willink knew that something wasn't right with the report, but it did not dawn on him until about ten minutes before he was to present his debrief. It was then he realized that he was to blame, and he should take responsibility for the failed operation. He stood in front of his commanding officer, master chief, investigating officer, and his men, including the SEALs who had been injured. As he was the one in command, he took full responsibility for the operation and went on to present new tactics and procedures to prevent an event like this from repeating itself.

His ego was bruised, but he gained the respect of his commanding officer and a deeper trust from the men he led in combat. When he took responsibility for his failures, the other soldiers took responsibility for theirs. Instead of losing respect for one another, they became responsible to each other as a team.

We Will Stop Depending on Others for Our Happiness

Back in the day, the crooner Dean Martin was the king of cool. Men wanted to be him, and women wanted to be with him. He recorded a hit song called "Everybody Loves Somebody." Martin's friend, Frank Sinatra, had previously recorded the song

---

26 Extreme Ownership | Jocko Willink | TEDxUniversityofNevada

as well. Martin's song went to number one on the music charts. Sadly, his personal life trailed far behind. Martin divorced three times; Sinatra did as well. Matrimony was only a temporary fix before they looked for something else to make them happy.

I'm not here to judge the two famous singers from another era. I'm emphasizing that happiness is elusive and can't be dependent on someone else. People, by nature, will let us down. Others can make a contribution to our happiness, but the responsibility for own happiness falls to us.

Jesus said we are happier when we give to others instead of expecting to receive from them. We should develop a network of friends and care for them deeply. We should each love and cherish our spouse and family. But realize that depending on them for personal happiness is unfair; this is not a need they can fulfill. Happiness is an inside job, and we are responsible for our success and happiness.

Take heart: God will help.

We Will Empower Ourselves to Solve Problems

Problems tend to be easily ignored when they are not our responsibility to fix. When we take responsibility, the wheels in our minds and hearts begin to turn. We become focused on and have more energy to come up with solutions. What previously did not concern us now becomes a preoccupation. We have got to get this done!

At Arlington Cemetery outside of Washington, DC, is the impressive Marine Corps Memorial. It commemorates the lives of American Marines who have served their country. The statue displays six World War II Marines raising an American flag over Mount Suribachi on the Pacific island of Iwo Jima. In the conquest of the island, over six thousand Marines were killed. The campaign put to test the Marine Corps slogan "Improvise, adapt, and overcome." Knowing it was their responsibility to capture the island, they refused to be defeated. Amid heavy resistance from Japanese soldiers and the harshest of conditions, they figured out a way and achieved victory. The memorial is a symbol of triumph through taking responsibility and figuring out how to get the job done.

"Write injuries in dust, benefits in marble," said Benjamin Franklin in the 1757 edition of his *Poor Richard's Almanack*. The benefits of responsibility change our lives for the better. Taking responsibility will give us reputations as problem-solvers and also provide great benefits to others.

WHAT IF WE DON'T TAKE RESPONSIBILITY?

Taking responsibility is a choice. We can choose to be responsible or irresponsible. What if we say no to becoming responsible? Think of the following consequences.

We Will Not Experience the Benefits Mentioned Above

Humans are creatures of will; sometimes we will, and sometimes we won't. The benefits of taking responsibility are massive but not guaranteed. There is something inside us that knows we should be responsible but then refuses to follow through. We wonder if it is really worth it. "What if I try and fail?" It seems easier to blame than to be responsible. Responsibility requires energy and hard work, faith, hope, and love. If we don't take responsibility for our lives, there is very little hope of experiencing the benefits mentioned above.

We Will Continue to Be Stuck

When I was a little boy, I got my head stuck in the railing of our townhouse apartment stairs. Don't ask how. I probably just wanted to see if I could push my head through the rails. Let's just say building codes were a little less stringent than today. I thought I could pry my way out, but my ears would not cooperate, and it hurt too much. I turned my head sideways, but my chin did not fit. My brother came by and laughed at me and then proclaimed the ultimate words of motivation: "I'm going to go tell Dad!"

Telling Dad, in my mind, meant getting into trouble and possibly being spanked for doing something I'm sure I was told not to do. With the little time I had before my father showed up, I mustered all of the strength that my five-year-old arms could manage, yanked apart the bars, and pulled my head out of the stair rails—probably leaving a little skin and hair behind. It hurt! When my dad showed up, I was calmly sitting on the stairs, smiling. I told Dad my brother was lying and hoped he would get in trouble.

Taking responsibility is hard. It may hurt, and we may lose a little hair, but it is better than regretting not being all God wants us to become.

Author Joelle Casteix is a survivor of child sexual abuse.[27] From age fifteen to seventeen, she was sexually abused by one of her high school teachers. He manipulated her emotions with flattery, time, gifts, and attention. She was too confused and scared to fight back. By the time the abuse was over, she was seventeen and pregnant, had a sexually transmitted disease, and felt utterly alone. To make matters worse, her friends and parents blamed her for the situation.

Feeling shame and self-loathing, Joelle started down a path of self-destruction: bad relationships, depression, isolation, self-hatred, and poor decisions. By the time she was twenty-seven, she was divorced and living at home with her father. Jobless, clinically depressed, and intermittently suicidal, she faced a future with little potential.

---

27 Joelle Casteix, *The Power of Responsibility*, TedxPasadenaWomen

Joelle did not *want* to be this way. She did not merely want to survive. She wanted to live and thrive. Her eureka moment came when she realized she did not *have* to be this way. She could change! She could stop blaming others and stop playing the victim. The key for her was to take responsibility for her life: past, present and future. It was not her fault for being abused, but it was her responsibility to move on.

When she took responsibility, she took back control of her life.

She explained, "I'm not talking about blame here. I'm talking about responsibility. It was not my fault that I was abused, but dwelling on the pain and blaming other people for my circumstances did nothing to help me heal. If I kept looking back, I could never move forward."

She stopped blaming her parents and high school friends for what had happened to her. She exposed the sexual predator and the high school that covered it up. She has become a worldwide advocate for the sexually abused and an in-demand speaker, in addition to being a wife and mother. All because she took responsibility!

The Condition May Get Worse

Greek philosopher Heraclitus said that one "cannot step into the same river twice." One motivation for taking responsibility is the awareness that life does not stand still. It continues to move forward. This means if we don't stay in step with it, life will get ahead of us, and we will get left behind. If we don't take responsibility for our weight, we will get heavier. If we don't take responsibility for our income, we will go deeper into debt. If we don't take responsibility to improve our skills, our value to the organization will probably decline. If we don't take responsibility to invest in relationships, we will lose friends and loved ones. If we don't take responsibility to pray, study the

Scripture, connect with a church, and lead a God-honoring life, we will not mature in our faith. As Paul wrote to the Galatians, "Do not be deceived, God is not mocked; whatsoever a man sows, that shall he also reap" (Galatians 6:7).

"The price of greatness is responsibility,"[28] said Winston Churchill. It was a much-needed mantra during the dark days of World War II as the Nazis were bombing civilians in London. The world today is a better place because the Allied forces took responsibility to fight for freedom.

CONCLUSION

The cost-benefit analysis is massively in favor of taking responsibility. The upside makes us more like Christ, and the downside makes us more like someone we don't want to be like! Our natural tendency wants to say, "It's my life, and I'll do what I want." Responsibility says, "It's my life, and I'll do what I should to glorify God and reach my full potential in Christ."

Take responsibility and reap the benefits of a better life!

CAN DO; GO DO

- ◊ Look over the benefits and consequences of responsibility listed in this chapter.
- ◊ Commit to taking full responsibility for your life and current situation.

---

28 https://winstonchurchill.org/old-site/learn/speeches-learn/the-price-of-greatness/

CHAPTER 8
HOW TO BECOME A RESPONSIBLE PERSON

"Create in me a clean heart, O God, and renew a right spirit within me."

PSALMS 51:10

"God does not flunk any of his children. He just re-enrolls them."

ADRIAN ROGERS

Knowing we should become a responsible person, as well as knowing *how* to become responsible, is critical to going in a better life direction. Knowing we should be responsible is an acknowledgement that it is up to us. Knowing how to be responsible is an action plan to get going in the right direction. Taking the following steps will go a long way in building the responsibility platform.

Recognize Our Problem

Have you been blaming others for your situation? Have you failed to follow through on your promises? Have you made excuses for your failures? If so, the common denominator is you.

Until we recognize the problem is ours, we will not have the desire to correct.

Look in the mirror and see the problem. Look up to God and take responsibility, and solutions will come.

Refuse to Blame

Too many people have been playing a losing hand in the card game of life. It keeps them spiritually and mentally poor while wishing their luck will change. The Christian life is not based around luck; it is based around loyalty to God and living in the grace and favor of his love. Refuse to blame, complain, mope, or make excuses. God has something better for us!

Repent of the Sin of Irresponsibility

King David had it all: power, riches, fame, family, respect, and much more. It was good to be king! He was also a man after God's own heart (Acts 13:22). Yet David acted irresponsibly. At a time when kings went out to war, David stayed home in the palace. While looking out from his rooftop, he saw the very beautiful Bathsheba bathing outside. He called for her, slept with her, and she became pregnant. In order to mask his sin, he had her husband Uriah sent to the front lines of the fighting, where he was killed in battle. The king thought he had gotten away with it, but God sent a prophet to confront David. David eventually admitted his destructive sinfulness, confessed, and repented of his actions.

God doesn't need to send a human prophet to tell us our sin. We have the teachings of the Bible and the convicting presence of the Holy Spirit. Confess to God the areas of your life for which you have not taken responsibility. Go to him in repentant prayer, and let him forgive the sin and restore the desire to live right by him. As was written in 1 John 1:9, "If we confess our sin He is faithful and just to forgive and cleanse us from all unrighteousness."

Renounce It and Let It Go

What we won't let go of won't let go of us. Release the mindset of irresponsibility. A batter who hits a home run is responsible to let go of the bat and run the bases in order for the run to count.

When we renounce something, we disavow our belief in it and loyalty to it. It is saying from the heart, "I don't believe that way anymore and will not act that way in the future!" Believe you died to being irresponsible, and renounce its control (Colossians 3:3).

Reach Up to Christ For Grace and Help

The psalmist said long ago, "I will lift my eyes upon the hills, from where does my help come? My help comes from the Lord, the maker of heaven and earth" (Psalms 121:1–2). Old habits die hard, and many times we are powerless to change them ourselves. We need God's help! To reach up to Christ is to constantly focus our mind on him to overcome the habits, hang-ups, and sins that can easily gain a foothold in our mind and body. We thereby rely on him to give us the power and strength we need.

Renew Our Minds

Our mind is renewed when we allow the Spirit of Christ to transform our way of thinking to line up with the Bible (Romans 8:2). Unrenewed thinking says responsibility is bad. Renewed thinking says responsibility is great. Unrenewed thinking says it is better to blame others. Renewed thinking says it is best to take ownership of our problems.

With a renewed mind, we begin to see ourselves as God sees us—children of God, made in his image, saved by the sacrifice of Christ, pardoned from sin, empowered by the Holy Spirit, more than conquerors, able to do all things through Christ who strengthens us!

Resolve to Replace Irresponsibility with Responsibility

The apostle Paul tells us that we are to put off the old self and put on the new, as if changing clothes (Ephesians 4:24). This signifies a conscious decision to believe and act a new way—the responsible way.

Irresponsibility (as well as any other sin) is the dirty suit of a past life. Pastor and author Dr. Adrian Rogers told a story comparing a man in dirty overalls with a man wearing a clean new suit. He said, "A man in a white suit will avoid the pig pen at all costs, because he doesn't want his suit stained with mud."[29]

Put on your clean white suit of responsibility.

Reframe How We Think about Responsibility

See responsibility as better than good. See it as the best way to live. Think of all the noble character traits we possess as responsible people: honesty, dependability, trustworthiness, reliability. Problem-solving, seeking solutions, and serving are our ways to success.

Relate Our Newfound Responsibility to Someone Else

Get an accountability partner. It can be one person, or it can be a small group of people. The key is to express our resolve to someone who can check with us on a regular basis and share in our progress. Can we become responsible without someone? Yes, but long-term, life-sustaining change is more likely to take hold if we have someone to hold us accountable.

In his book *Change or Die*, author Alan Deutschman chronicles the lives of people, from heart patients to heroin addicts, who accomplished sustained life change. He concludes that the first key to change is to "form a new, emotional relationship with a person or community that inspires and

---

29 Adrian Rogers, *A Man of His Word, DVD Curriculum Calling Men to Integrity and Leadership* (Dallas, Sampson Resources).

sustains hope."[30] That's an accountability partner!

Rest In God's Love

Psalms 116:7 says, "Return to your rest, my soul, for the Lord has been good to you."

Taking responsibility for our lives is a spiritual exercise as much as it is a personal decision. There is a war going on in our hearts: a battle between good and evil. It can lead to weariness of the heart and soul. Our success has much to do with our taking responsibility. Resting in God's love has everything to do with what Jesus did on the cross. Jesus encourages us to come to him for rest. We don't do anything for it. We rest in it.

CONCLUSION

Start where you are and take 100 percent responsibility for your life!

We are victors, not victims; winners, not whiners; battlers, not blamers. We seek excellence, not excuses. We want God's power, not self-pity. We are empowered, not entitled. We are not inferior, inadequate, unable, worthless, or unworthy. We are reliable, dependable, response-able children of God. We may have failed in the past, but we are not failures. We know how to be responsible. Responsibility is our character trait, and we honor our word and see our commitments through until they have been completed!

A Prayer for Responsibility

"Dear Father, gracious and merciful in every way. I come to you acknowledging that I have sinned against you by not taking

---

30 Alan Deutschman, *Change or Die* (New York: Harper, 2007) 14.

responsibility for my life. I have blamed others and complained about my circumstances. I ask you to forgive me and help me to take complete responsibility for my life. In Jesus' name. Amen."

CAN DO; GO DO

- ◇ Review the steps involved in realizing responsibility.
- ◇ Renew your commitment to being responsible.
- ◇ Recite the prayer above, in faith and from the heart.

CHAPTER 9
TRUING THE LIFE WHEEL

The intersections of life must align with our faith and ambitions if we are to reach our potential in Christ.

"He gives to all life, breath, and all things."

ACTS 17:25

"Your future does not equal your past. Tomorrow is full of possibility you can access right now."

MICHAEL HYATT

My daughter and I liked to ride bikes together. When we were on vacation in California, we rode over the Golden Gate Bridge. We breezed through the fog and mist while looking down below at the San Francisco Bay. We stopped in the middle and took selfies. It is a fond memory of a shared experience. The wind blowing back one's hair while trekking across a smooth road or trail is a great feeling.

One of our rides in Hilton Head, South Carolina, was not so smooth. Chelsea was a fairly new biker and still warming up her Tour de France skills from the seat of her rental bike. We were riding around at the resort, and she was a little ahead of me when she ran out of sidewalk. Not knowing what to do, and not thinking about hitting the brakes, she cycled through the grass and smacked into the side of a building. I can still picture in my mind the sight of her little body coming to a very sudden stop. Thankfully, she was not hurt, but she was understandably finished riding bikes for the day. We returned the bikes without mentioning the incident.

A bicycle with perfectly round wheels is a great ride: smooth and responsive to the turn of the handlebar. But when it is out of round—say, as the result of hitting a curb or a building—the ride is bumpy and rough, if not impossible. If the wheel is not too badly damaged, a bicycle-repair technician can use a truing tool to adjust the tension on the spokes. This makes the wheel round again and returns it to proper balance, or "trueness."

The decision to take responsibility for one's life is like a truing tool for the heart. It is an important, positive mind shift for reaching our God-given potential through Christ, swinging our position from victim to victor. It recalibrates our mental focus from blaming others to looking to God for his help and grace in living a fruitful life before him.

Life is multidimensional. We have family and friends, work, church, hobbies, finances, and many other things that vie for our attention. A fair question to ask is "What are the areas of life I should be concerned with?" I have listed eight major categories of the life wheel that we should be aware of and in which we might seek to invest our time and attention.

Picture in your mind a wheel with eight spokes. At the center is a hub that anchors them. The spokes represent the typical categories of life. The hub represents God. The outside of the wheel is life, which roles along, sometimes smooth, sometimes bumpy (see diagram on page 93).

GOD IS THE HUB

Before discussing the categories of the life wheel, it is essential to remember that God must be at the center of life. He is the hub of the life wheel, the center to which the spokes are anchored. Jesus told us to "seek *first* the kingdom of God and his righteousness, and all these things will be added to you" (Matthew 6:33; emphasis added). This means we should place every area of our life under the direction and control of Christ. When making decisions, our first considerations should be "Does this honor/glorify God? Is my decision true to Scripture? Do I believe this is God's will for my life?" If the answer is yes to these questions and consistent with the teaching of the Bible, then go forward in faith. Christ must be all, and in all (Colossians 3:11).

Preachers and teachers have used pictures and diagrams to show how God should be first. Some picture a rectangular box with God at the top and other categories in descending order—usually something in the order of God, family, then work. This is not necessarily wrong, but I think the wheel is better because it shows how all of life revolves around God. Jesus told the disciples, "And you shall love the Lord your God with all your heart and with all your soul and with all your mind and with all your strength" (Mark 12:30 ESV).

When God is in the center, he touches every component of life.

SPOKES IN THE WHEEL

Social psychologists and life coaches attempt to help people set goals by targeting categories out of which life is lived. Some have more categories, some less. The objective of the exercise is to bring awareness to our lives and achieve growth and balance in each category. The following areas are key for understanding the "all things" of Philippians 4:13.

Spiritual

Paul explained to the Corinthian church, "Now we have not received the spirit of the world, but the Spirit who is from God, that we might know the things freely given to us by God" (1 Corinthians 2:12).

The moment a person trusts Christ as Savior and Lord, they become spiritually alive to God and indwelt by the Holy Spirit. We are spiritual beings in a physical body.

The Bible makes many references to the spiritual nature of life: we are in a spiritual battle (Ephesians 6:12), we must put on spiritual armor (Ephesians 6:11), we are to be filled with the Holy Spirit (Ephesians 5:18) and walk in the Spirit (Galatians 5:16), our minds are to be spiritually renewed (Ephesians 4:23), and we are instructed to "quench not the Holy Spirit" (1 Thessalonians 5:19). Developing spiritually is essential for a well-rounded life.

I count the spiritual first because, as followers of Christ, we are expected to grow in the faith through spiritual development. How do we develop spiritually? Bible study and meditation, prayer, community, worship, giving, and serving are some key activities God uses to conform us to the image of Christ (Romans 8:29).

Physical

Paul also wrote, "Do you not know that your body is the temple of the Holy Spirit who is in you, whom you have from God, and you are not your own? For you were bought with a price, therefore glorify God in your body, and in your spirit, which are God's." (1 Corinthians 6:19–20).

We are to take responsibility for our physical body. Staying healthy honors God and helps us feel better. People who maintain a healthy body and reduce stress have more energy and a better mental disposition. A healthy lifestyle is a good thing.

In the context of 1 Corinthians 6, there are two areas in particular the apostle Paul draws attention to: overindulgence—or gluttony—and sexual purity.

Overindulgence/Gluttony

Someone has said, "Men don't have hobbies; they have vices." I believe that's an oversimplification, but it does carry a strong warning about how easy it is to overindulge. A few extra helpings of food over time and, consequently, two out of three Americans are considered overweight or obese.[31] A little wine at dinner or a beer during the game can quickly turn into overconsumption and lead to drunkenness and addiction. We are called to use our bodies for the glory of God and not abuse them through self-indulgence.

Sexual Purity

"For this is the will of God, even your sanctification, that you should abstain from sexual immorality; that each of you should know how to control your body in purity and honor," Paul told the Thessalonian church (1 Thessalonians 4:3–4).

God has made us sexual creatures. It is a natural desire. Like any desire, it can be abused. This happens when we seek to gratify our flesh in ways that do not honor God. We live in a sex-crazed world, and temptation seems to be everywhere. The good news is that purity is possible through the power of Christ.

God has given us a way to express ourselves sexually—through marriage between a man and a woman. Marriage is a beautiful expression of committed love and a mysterious symbol

---

31 https://www.niddk.nih.gov/health-information/health-statistics/overweight-obesity

of Christ and his relation to the church (Ephesians 5:32). Sexual self-control is worth the wait.

Many studies show the benefits of a healthy body and the positive effects on longevity and well-being. Our body is a temple of the Holy Spirit. We should treat it right.

Emotional

Proverbs 16:32 explains, "He who is slow to anger is better than the mighty, and he who rules his spirit than the one who conquers a city."

We live in a culture that has replaced "I think" with "I feel." Sadly, it's as if feelings, and not facts, have become the validation of truth.

Healthy emotions are good. They display our love, passion, exuberance, empathy, and compassion. Jesus loved, laughed, got angry (yet did not sin), and felt compassion and emotional hurt. God has made us to feel deeply.

Unhealthy emotions are harmful. On one end of the spectrum, they can cause us to lash out in anger or develop compulsive habits due to lack of impulse control. On the other end of the spectrum, unhealthy emotions can cause a person to be sullen, withdrawn, discouraged, and depressed. Unbridled emotions can lead to negative obsession that causes us to fixate on people or problems. We can become bitter, envious, spiteful, hateful, obsessive, and petty.

A few lines from Rudyard Kipling's poem "If" form a helpful reminder:

> If you can keep your head when all about you are losing theirs and blaming you . . .
> If you can force your heart and nerve and sinew to serve your turn long after they are gone . . .
> If all men count with you, but none too much . . .

Yours is the Earth and everything that's in it,
And—which is more—you'll be a Man, my son![32]

People who can manage their emotions and tune into the emotions of others increase their ability to succeed; they have emotional intelligence, or EQ. The ability to be "others oriented" while keeping oneself emotionally healthy signals emotional maturity, which is part of balancing the wheel of life.

Intellectual/Educational

The first textbook for Pilgrim children in America was the Bible. Many years later, the original charter of Harvard College stated that the purpose of the institution was for "the education of the English and Indian youth of this country in knowledge and godliness."[33] The Christian faith encourages learning by believing: "The Lord gives wisdom and from His mouth comes knowledge and understanding" (Proverbs 2:6).

Part of a well-rounded life is continuing to grow in our knowledge of God, ourselves, our profession, the world, and people. Learning doesn't end when we graduate from school. We should be students of life and lifelong learners. What set Daniel, Shadrach, Meshach, and Abednego apart from others? They devoted themselves to God, and God "gave them knowledge and intelligence in every branch of literature and wisdom; Daniel even understood all kinds of visions and dreams" (Daniel 1:17).

Devout Christian and hall-of-fame motivational speaker Charlie "Tremendous" Jones said, "You will be the same person in five years as you are today except for the people you meet and the books you read."[34] Dedicate yourself to learning the right things from the right people. Get into a Bible study where you

---

32 Rudyard Kipling, "If": https://poets.org/poem/if
33 https://guides.library.harvard.edu/c.php?g=880222&p=6323072
34 https://tremendousleadership.com/pages/charlie

can learn the Bible. Train in your work and become the best at it you can. Learning comes before earning and is an investment in a well-developed life.

Reading is fundamental, but not everyone likes to read. Thankfully, we live in a world of multiple informational options. Take advantage of podcasts, instructional videos, and downloads. Work whatever way works best for you. "Leaders are feeders": that is, they feed their mind good content from different sources. Some learn by doing, some by watching, and some by listening. The well-rounded person will take advantage of all the outlets available to them.

It is also wise to be careful of what we take into our minds. It is easy to waste countless hours playing video games, looking at social media, or watching television. A little recreation is one thing, but don't feed on intellectual junk food! As Colossians 3:2 says, "Set your mind on things above, not on earth below."

Because we have the mind of Christ, the wise follower will develop their intellect to the glory of God.

Relational

Relationships are rewarding. They give us an opportunity to love and be loved. Community is a place where we can be accepted and nurtured. Life is better together. Relationships can also be challenging, whether they be with a spouse, children, relatives, friends, neighbors, coworkers, colleagues, or the church (if I missed someone, please add your own). Any way we look at it, there are a lot of people to get along with. It is not always easy, but it is worth it.

God is relational. He exists as Father, Son, and Holy Spirit. He also created us to have fellowship with him. He created man and woman to love each other, marry, and procreate. He created the family to perpetuate humanity. Families became towns where people could live together in community. Rules and laws were made to protect each other. Towns became nations where people could live together with a distinctive identity and culture.

God created the church: his people, living out their faith together in community. One reason why God gave us the Bible is so we can learn to love and live together with him and each other. God created us to be relational!

Two relational areas that are particularly important are spouse and children. Neglecting these relationships can lead to family dysfunction and divorce. Husbands and wives are meant to build each other up in love and respect, and not tear each other apart. Parents are meant to see their children as a blessing from the Lord and raise them in the nurture and admonition of the Lord (Ephesians 5:22–6:4).

Aristotle said, "Man, by nature, is a political animal." "Political" comes from the Greek word "*polis*," which is understood to be a group of people living in community. He believed that because people could speak to one another and reason together, community was the natural order of things.

Part of the "all things" God wants us to do is to grow our relationship skills. We are to learn to love, respect, appreciate, care for, interact with, and serve one another.

Vocational

Paul told the Colossians, "Whatever you do, do your work heartily as to the Lord, not to men, knowing that from the Lord you will receive an inheritance. For it is the Lord Christ whom you serve" (Colossians 3:23–24).

A global poll conducted by the Gallup organization revealed that a mere 15 percent of the world's billion-plus workers are "engaged" or satisfied at their job. The percentage in the United States is somewhat better at 30 percent but still far from a majority.[35] Lack of engagement is a cause of lower productivity

---

35 https://news.gallup.com/opinion/chairman/212045/world-broken-

and lack of excellence in one's work.

It seems most people are dissatisfied with their work—the very place they spend most of their waking hours. Our work matters to God and is one of the major components of life. God created Adam and Eve to "tend" the Garden of Eden. From the beginning, we were created to be employed in productive activity. We must take responsibility to glorify God in our work, career, or vocation.

Financial

God provides much admonition in the area of finances, both positive and negative: Moses said, "You shall remember the Lord your God, for it is he who gives you power to get wealth" (Deuteronomy 8:18 ESV). King Solomon said, "The rich and the poor have this in common; the Lord is the Maker of them all" (Proverbs 22:2 NIV). Jesus said, "You cannot serve God and mammon" (Matthew 6:24). The apostle Paul reminded us, "The love of money is the root of all evil" (1 Timothy 6:10).

God is not opposed to money. He knows we need it to live—to buy groceries and clothes and pay the mortgage. Society is based on the monetary transaction of goods and services.

When it comes to making a living, it is no sin to be paid well for the work we do. But how we handle our finances can be a millstone around our necks or a stepping stone to living a good life. As financial advisor Dave Ramsey informed us, "In fact, if you don't get your money under control, this one area can destroy your whole life."[36]

I would like nothing better than to take my place among the idle rich. Sitting on a yacht with a captain and crew catering to my every whim seems like a great life. I also know the raw

---

workplace
36 Dave Ramsey, *Dave Ramsey's Complete Guide to Money* (Brentwood, TN: Lampo Press, 2010).

pursuit of more money and things can draw my heart away from God. The wisdom of the pursuit of wealth is that it must be tempered with honest ambition and a generous heart. As eighteenth-century English cleric John Wesley said, "If those who 'gain all they can,' and 'save all they can,' will likewise 'give all they can'; then, the more they gain, the more they will grow in grace, and the more treasure they will lay up in heaven."[37]

Deciding what kind of lifestyle we desire to live and finding a career that can support it is important. It is not the use of money but the mismanagement of money that gets us into trouble. To paraphrase a common saying, "If money talks to me, it usually says goodbye." Financial stewardship is a great responsibility.

Recreational/Avocation

Recreational activities and hobbies can be a wholesome diversion. They help us unwind and redirect us from the monotony of life, as well as allowing us to socialize and make new friends. We are blessed to live in a time that affords us some leisure.

Find something that interests you and you enjoy doing. My friend Calvin Miller was a preacher, professor, and prolific writer. He also loved to paint. Placing colors on a canvas relaxed him and gave him a mental vacation in order to recharge his mind. King David ruled Israel and yet made time to play the harp. Find some "me" time to relax and recharge. A good vacation is important too. Sometimes it's good to get away, relax, and refresh. Recreate responsibly.

---

37 https://www.resourceumc.org/en/content/john-wesley-on-giving

KEEP THE LIFE WHEEL ROLLING ALONG

How well rounded is your life? In what areas would you like to make progress? I would recommend taking some time to look over the areas of the life wheel and committing to being more responsible to improve in areas that need attention. As you do, keep in mind the following tips.

Every Life Has Bumps, and the Wheel Can Get out of Balance

Life happens. Pick any area of life, and there will be times of abundance and times of lack, times of joy and times of pain. It is through the struggle and the suffering that we learn we can do all things through Christ who strengthens us. We live in the promise that even when the wheels fall off, he will never leave us or forsake us (Hebrews 13:5).

We Can Improve in Any Area

Paul encouraged the Christians of Galatia, "And let us not grow weary in doing good, for in due time we shall reap if we do not lose heart" (Galatians 6:10).

By God's grace and focused action, we can grow any area of life. It may take time and perseverance, but we can do it! Live in hope! The past doesn't equal the future. We may be one prayer away from turning the corner.

Each Area Can Affect the Other

A kaleidoscope is a tube with mirrors and angled glass with different colors. Looking through one end of the tube and turning the other end changes the angle of the glass and presents an ever-changing pattern. Areas of our lives can seem like a kaleidoscope: growing in one area can change the dynamic in another.

For instance, if our bodies are in pain, that can affect our emotions. We will not feel like praying, developing our intellect, or going to work. Or if we are having marital issues, it can cause a lack of productivity at work as well as physical sickness due to stress. Also, every parent knows the condition of being preoccupied with a sick child or distracted by their not doing well.

On the other hand, a pay raise can allow one to better provide for the needs of their family and reduce some emotional stress. Becoming more physically fit can release endorphins that lead to a more positive outlook and well-being. Spiritual disciplines draw us closer to God and strengthen relationships within the church.

Personal Growth Honors God

Some believe personal growth is self-centered. I think it depends on the heart. As I've mentioned, if "self-help" or personal development is undertaken so that one can succeed without God, then there is a problem. But if we want to reach our God-given potential through Christ, then we should strive to be our best for God.

Paul said, "We make it our aim to be pleasing to Him. For we must all appear before the judgment seat of Christ, so that each one may receive the reward for what he has done in the body, whether good or evil" (2 Corinthians 5:9–10). Biblical personal growth equals Christian maturity and practical sanctification.

CONCLUSION

Cyclists can ride a bike with one, two, or even three broken spokes, but not for very long or very far. And when a spoke breaks, the bike gets wobbly, and the rider is constantly preoccupied with whether the tire will collapse and the bike will crash.

Take responsibility for the spokes in your life wheel.

CAN DO; GO DO

◊ Look over the categories of the life wheel. Would you add any?

◊ Pick one or two areas and determine one way you will improve.

GOD

- VOCATIONAL
- SPIRITUAL
- RELATIONAL
- INTELLECTUAL
- PHYSICAL
- EMOTIONAL
- FINANCIAL
- AVOCATIONAL

SECTION 3

"CAN"

A strong *belief* in God, ourselves, and what we are doing is essential to reaching our God-given dreams

"I **can** do all things through Christ who strengthens me."

CHAPTER 10
EVERYONE HAS IT; SOME KNOW IT AND GROW IT

Reaching our God-given potential involves a growing faith.

"If you can believe, all things are possible to him who believes...."
"I believe, help my unbelief."

MARK 9:23–25

"The one who thinks they can and the one who thinks they can't are both right."

We have taken responsibility for our lives. We have put the past behind us and are looking forward to where God is leading us. Fantastic! But where is he leading? How will we get there? And how will we know when we have arrived? These are questions of belief, or faith questions.

The second word of Philippians 4:13 is "can." It is a word of faith or belief.

Everyone has faith, even if they don't think so. If we fly in an airplane, we believe the plane and pilot are competent to fly and land safely at our destination. When we are driving in a car, we believe the car coming toward us will stay on their side of the road. When we are sick, we see a doctor we probably do not know and are prescribed a medicine we are not sure how to pronounce to cure an illness we are not 100 percent sure we have! We cannot prove any of these things until after the fact. We have to believe them before we see results.

Everyone has faith, but faith must be devoted, developed, and directed. Faith is *devoted* when we trust Jesus to be our personal Savior and Lord. Faith is *developed* as we follow Christ in discipleship. Faith is *directed* when we believe God is leading us to take action to pursue our God-given dreams. God has given us faith to believe. It is our responsibility to cooperate with him and develop it. Faith is like a muscle; the more we use it, the stronger it becomes. How is faith developed?

THE B-I-B-L-E IS THE FAITH BOOK FOR ME

We learned the song in Sunday school and Vacation Bible School: "The B-I-B-L-E, yes, that's the book for me. I stand alone on the Word of God, the B-I-B-L-E." The teachings of the Bible are the firm foundation for faith and life; they are God's primary means of developing our faith. As Paul wrote to the Romans, "Faith comes by hearing, and hearing by the Word of God" (Romans 10:17).

In the Bible, we learn the nature of God—that he is all powerful, all loving, all knowing, and everywhere at once. We also learn how he performed miracles to help his people. We learn in Scripture how to honor God in the way we live and think. Additionally, we learn that God is for us (Romans 8:31–39) and wants us to succeed. We also learn from the Scripture that God is reconciling the world to himself through Jesus Christ (John 3:16).

How is faith developed through the Bible? By massive exposure to it! According to a 2017 survey conducted by Lifeway research, 87 percent of Americans own a Bible. They have positive feelings toward the Book and believe it gives helpful information for living. However, more than half of Americans have read little or none of the Bible![38] No wonder our faith toward God is weak.

Psalms 119:105 says, "Thy Word is a lamp unto my feet and a light unto my path"; having a Bible and not reading it is like having a high-powered searchlight and never turning it on. When we get into the Bible, the Bible will get into us. The following principles in regard to Scripture will help grow our faith.

Receive It as God's True Word

James said, "And receive with meekness the implanted word, which is able to save your souls" (James 1:21).

The Bible is God's truth, whether one believes it or not. In order for us to be changed by it, we must approach it with a believing heart. We must be open to letting God change us through the Holy Spirit in applying Scripture to every area of life. Receiving his Word means coming to God and saying, "I trust you. I follow you. I believe you." We must believe God's Word is at the root of living in order to see the fruits of success.

Hear It

The author of Psalms begs, "My people, *hear* my words, listen to the instruction of my mouth . . . tell them to your children . . . so that they may put their confidence in God" (Psalms 78:1,7, emphasis added)

When I was younger, I would listen to the Bible on cassette tapes. It was much better for my soul than most of the music on the radio. Today, we have so much access to ways of listening, such as radio, television, internet, phone apps, and streaming. Make the choice to turn off the other stuff and listen to Scripture.

---

38 http://www.bpnews.net/48743/study-americans-fond-of-bible-but-how-many-read-it

You can download the Youversion Bible app for free.[39] I use it sometimes to listen to Scripture while I am at the gym or while I fall asleep.

Another way of hearing the Word of God is through good Bible preaching and teaching. This is why attendance in a Bible-believing and preaching church is so important. What we listen to will influence us, and if we are not listening to the good stuff, the God stuff, we will be influenced by the world. There are many good preachers. For recommendations, ask your pastor whom he listens to.

Read It

As the saying goes, "Reading is fundamental." Jesus said, "Man does not live by bread alone, but by every word that proceeds from the mouth of God" (Matthew 4:4). Hearing the Word is good, but sometimes our thoughts wander in and out. Think about the number of times you have listened to the same song and still don't know all the words. It is because we are usually not focusing. Reading is more active. We have to pick up the book and look at the words on the pages and think about what we are seeing and comprehending.

According to a study by Crossway, it takes about 75.5 hours to read the entire Bible, both Old and New Testaments. That means a typical reader can enjoy the entire Bible in a year by reading just twelve minutes per day.[40] What better use of our time than to grow our faith through being in the Book?

Study It

Paul wrote Timothy, "Study and show yourself approved unto God, a workman that needs not be ashamed, rightly

---

39 https://www.youversion.com/the-bible-app/
40 https://www.crossway.org/articles/infographic-you-can-read-more-of-the-bible-than-you-think/

dividing the word of truth" (2 Timothy 2:15).

For faith to grow, we must spend time with Scripture and go deeper than surface reading. We must study to find out not only what Scripture says but also what it means.

When I started reading the Bible, I was both amazed and perplexed. I was amazed at what was obviously clear and straightforward. I was also perplexed by many passages because I did not understand the meaning of the text. I needed help. Thankfully, my dad let me borrow his study Bible. My knowledge of Scripture grew from reading Scripture. My understanding grew through using a study Bible. My faith grew through spending time studying Scripture.

A good study Bible will give background into each book of the Bible and how particular verses are understood. It will also provide help with cultural and grammatical considerations in working with the text. God has provided us with study Bibles and Bible study tools! Invest in them, and your faith will grow exponentially. The better we understand the Bible, the more confidence we will have in the truth of what it says, and that leads to stronger faith!

In addition to personal Bible study, we should also be in a Bible study group. This can be a Sunday school class, home group, work group, or formal classroom or online education. As Proverbs 27:17 puts it, "As iron sharpens iron, one person can sharpen another."

When we study the Bible with other people, we receive the benefit of their insight into Scripture. We are encouraged when we hear how they have applied Scripture to their lives and developed in their faith.

Memorize It

The author of Psalms tells God, "Your word I have treasured in my heart, that I might not sin against You" (119:11).

God tells us to renew our minds (Romans 12:2). That is, we are to let go of the junk thoughts that society and culture condition us to believe and replace them with the truth of God. Satan uses negative thoughts and our misguided emotions to deceive us and confuse us. Scripture memorization is a defense against the devil's deceptive tactics; it is the secret sauce to faith building. Recalling Scripture from memory and reciting it out loud will encourage us as we pursue our God-given dreams and bring courage when we are tempted to doubt. We are counseled by God to let his word live in us abundantly (Colossians 3:16).

When I was a teenager, I purchased the Navigators' Topical Memory System. It contained Bible verses written on little cards and a vinyl pouch in which to keep them. I memorized two Bible verses a week until I completed all sixty verses. I would keep the pouch in my pocket and pull it out and read the verse in my spare time. I placed it at my work station and would look at and recite the verse throughout the day. My boss did not mind; he saw improvement in my work performance! Through the years, I have quoted the verses frequently. The value of Scripture memory pays massive spiritual dividends in proportion to the time invested.

Take this challenge: memorize Philippians 4:13 and say it out loud ten times a day: "I can do all things through Christ who strengthens me." You will have more faith in God and his working in you, and more willingness to try new things.

Meditate

Joshua 1:8 reads, "This Book of the Law shall not depart from your mouth, but you shall meditate on it, both day and night, so that you may be careful to do according to all that is in it. For then you will make your way prosperous. Then you will have good success" (ESV).

Joshua meditated on God's Word and had the faith and courage to lead the children of Israel into the Promised Land.

To meditate means to ponder the meaning—to actively engage the text for insight. It is deep reflection in a quest for better understanding of God and his way.

King David, the lion-killing, giant-slaying, enemy-defeating warrior-king of Israel, strengthened his faith through this kind of reflection. David's prescription for being blessed by God was meditating on Scripture: "His delight is in the Law of the Lord, and in his law he does meditate both day and night . . . and whatsoever he does shall prosper" (Psalms 1:2,3). "Prosper" can be understood as a synonym for success. Faith grows when we spend time with God, meditating in his Word.

Apply

Jesus advised his disciples, "Be doers of the Word, and not hearers only, deceiving yourselves" (James 1:22).

One of the keys to strengthening our faith is to act on what we know. We are to stand *on* the Word and walk *in* obedience to it. "Just do it" is more than a sports apparel motto. It is a spiritual brand we wear for strengthening belief.

D. L. Moody said, "The Bible was not meant for our information but for our transformation"—wise words from someone who expressed incredible faith in God and the power of the gospel. Use the tools to mine the riches of God's Word.

PRAYER

The passage from Mark shown at the beginning of this chapter comes from the story of Jesus casting out an unclean spirit from a child.

The child's father brought him to Jesus's disciples, but they could not rid the child of the evil spirit. The man called out to

Jesus and asked him if he could do something. Jesus reminded the man to put his trust in God and have faith. The man responded that he had faith but needed more. Jesus honored the man's plea and answered by healing the son. Later, the disciples came to Jesus and asked him why they could not cast out the unclean spirit. Jesus responded that the particular kind of spirit could only be cast out by prayer[41] (Mark 9:29).

Notice the man in the story did not have perfect faith. He did not even have great faith. But he did have enough faith to talk to Jesus and ask him to heal his child. Though he was weak in faith, he knew Jesus could help him believe better! The same is true with us. As we talk to God in prayer, our relationship with him grows stronger, and so does our faith.

Prayer is talking to God reverently and honestly. In prayer, we voice our admiration to God. We confess our sins and weaknesses, hurts, and hang-ups. We focus on the greatness of God and his power to forgive our sin, heal our heart, and help us in life. We also voice our requests to him through the authority of Jesus. God knows our hearts and our needs before we ask. Prayer is the spiritual safe space where God comforts us in private and gives us confident faith in public.

The nature of prayer is not merely to get something from God. Prayer is to grow closer to God. As we spend time with God, we understand him better and trust him more. Our faith grows as well. Just as bigger and better fruit results from staying connected to the branch, greater faith is the result of abiding in Christ (John 15:4). As the old preacher Oswald Chambers said, "Prayer does not fit us for the greater works; prayer is the greater work."[42] Work on spending more time with God in prayer, and more faith will follow.

---

41 Some versions add "and fasting." Both are good.
42 https://utmost.org/classic/greater-works-classic/

DOUBT OUR DOUBTS

James said, "If any of you lacks wisdom, let him ask of God, who gives liberally and without reproach. But let him ask in faith, without doubting" (James 1:5–6).

Doubt is a roadblock to faith. It keeps great ideas from germinating and can stymie the greatest movements. Doubt can keep the greatest questions from being asked and the greatest answers from being understood. Doubt knocks the "try" out of "triumph." Doubt destroys. It has been said that faith moves mountains and doubt creates them.

There are many factors that condition us to doubt: Our sinful nature shows us our capacity for wrong. Life's disappointments can knock the "want to" out of us. Negative people tell us it can't be done. Personal failures keep us from thinking things will get better. These and other forces conspire to tell us we "can't" instead of "can."

There is a legendary tale about Robert Fulton I like to tell. In 1807, Robert Fulton launched the first steamboat, the *Claremont*. It traveled 150 miles up the Hudson River from New York City to Albany in record time. Fulton proved the steamboat was not only useful but also profitable, and a new era in shipping was born.

Not everyone who assembled to watch the steamer's maiden voyage was a fan of Fulton, or of steam engine ships. It is said that before the ship set sail, there was a man at the dock yelling, "It will never start! It will never start." The engineer fired up the engines, and smoke began billowing from the stack. The mooring lines were released, and the captain set sail. As the ship left port, the same man was heard yelling, "It will never stop! It will never stop!"

I don't know if the story is true to fact, but it is true to life. We live in a world of doubters. The good news is we don't have to be counted among them.

How do we doubt our doubts? First, imagine how God can use you to make your goals possible. Think about all the ways it can work instead of all the ways it can't.

Second, think long and hard about what it will take to get it done instead of believing it can't be done. Think about it repeatedly, multiple times a day. Pray about it regularly. When we begin to think about the "how," it can open up our minds to the possibility of success, as well as fostering the beginnings of a plan.

Third, think deeply about the good you will accomplish by having what God has placed in your heart come to fruition. Picture the results in your mind as if they have already happened. Picture the people who will benefit from what you would like to see happen. Reframe negative doubts with a positive "can do"! Ask God for grace to doubt your doubts.

FAITH-FILLED PEOPLE

My friend Floyd was naturally optimistic. I asked him why he was so positive, and he said, "It's just my nature."

I asked, "Floyd, do you listen to motivational tapes?"

He said, "I can't listen to them because they get my confidence so amped up I just want to go out and do crazy stuff."

Floyd was what I like to call a faith-filled man. And his faith would spill over to others.

Some people have the spiritual gift of faith (1 Corinthians 12:9). It is a special ability given by God to accomplish great tasks. There are not many in the church with the "gift" of faith, but every church, I believe, has some. Find them. Hang around them. Let their faith inspire you.

In pursuing our God-given dreams, we need to develop a support system of people who believe in us and what God wants us to do. These are people who will encourage us when we tend to doubt or when we feel we are not making progress. These are people who will pray for us when the task is hard and we want to give up. We don't need many, but we all need some, and the more the merrier; after all, "two is better than one . . . and a three-fold cord is not easily broken (Ecclesiastes 4:9,11). Moses had Aaron to support him. David had Jonathan. Paul was encouraged by Barnabas.

One word of advice: be careful and stay away from negative people who want to tamp down your faith and pour cold water on the fire of your God-given goals and dreams. Just like some have the gift of faith, there are others who have developed the "gift" of criticism. They are quick to say how it can't be done instead of believing it is possible. These are "can't do" instead of "can do" people. Don't let them set up a tent in your camp.

People can influence us for good or for ill. Get around faith-filled people! Have as friends people who can build you up and not tear you down—people who believe in Christ and believe he is working in you, because "bad company corrupts good morals" (1 Corinthians 15:33).

Our destinies are too valuable to be influenced by dream stealers.

HAVE A "WITH GOD ALL THINGS ARE POSSIBLE" MINDSET

Matthew 19:26 declares, "With man this is impossible, but with God all things are possible."

People tend not to try things they believe will have a bad result. Why invest the time and energy on something we think is doomed to fail? Why spend time and emotional energy on people we believe will abandon us? Why invest money in companies that may go bankrupt? The pragmatic person would rightly say we shouldn't.

But what if we approached life with the foundational attitude that whatever God calls us to do, he will cause to work for good—his good? That is a can-do, cannot fail attitude. It is a faith-growing, life-conquering mindset. It is the mindset that says, "With God, all things are possible." This mindset is like a batter who can see the strings on a fastball and knows he has a chance of hitting a home run. It is like a ballerina who can picture performing the perfect dance in her head—the twists, twirls, and jumps—and still land on her toes.

Jonathan, the son of King Saul, had this kind of attitude. The Israelites were at war with the Philistines. Jonathan decided to go to the enemy's garrison and check on their movement. He said to his armor bearer, "Let's go to the garrison of these [Philistines]. It may be the Lord will work for us, for nothing can hinder the Lord from saving by many or by few" (1 Samuel 14:6 ESV). God delivered the Philistines into the hands of Jonathan. He and his armor bearer quickly killed twenty men, and the rest of the enemy fled in a panic.

Jonathan could have talked himself out of seeing the good hand of God working for him. He could have said, "It's too risky," "I need back-up," or "This is not the best time to fight." Instead, he trusted in a good God who can cause all things to work together for his good.

Psychologist and educator Dr. Carolyn Dweck authored *Mindset: The New Psychology of Success*. The book has become a bestseller with sales approaching two million copies. When Dr. Dweck was a young woman, she wanted all the things that life could give her: a glamorous career, a great husband, and recognition. She believed these things would validate who she was. She married a great husband, but he was a "work in progress." She had a great career, but it came with many challenges. Nothing she strived for seemed to come easy. Nor was she "satisfied" with where she was in life.

All of this changed when she and one of her doctoral students were having a conversation about why some students were caught up in proving their ability, while other students could let go and learn. Dr. Dweck delineated what she considered to be two mindsets: a fixed mindset and a growth mindset.

A fixed mindset holds that ability is predetermined or "fixed" and the best someone can do is go as far as they can with their natural gifts and talents. This mindset is overly concerned about mistakes and failures due to a belief that personal validation only comes from getting things right all the time. Achievement, in this way of thinking, merely validates what someone already has the ability to do.

A growth mindset, on the other hand, believes that people can change and develop. They can grow and achieve better through faith, desire, effort, learning, and good teaching.

Dr. Dweck realized her fixed mindset was keeping her from being satisfied with where she was and what she thought she had in life. She only saw what she believed was right or wrong in her life, with no hope of change. She changed her mind to a growth mindset: the belief that she could grow in her marriage and career and that effort is part of the journey. Satisfaction came by choosing to change the way she looked at her situation.

Faith grows when we open our minds to the possibility that God can do something to us, with us, and through us. We have to open our minds to the truth that God's power is greater than our limitations. We are not trapped but rather free to grow into all God has for us. When we believe that all things are possible with God, we have moved the faith needle in the right direction.

ENDURING TRIALS WITH JOY

James 1:2 encourages Christians, "Count it all joy my brethren, when you encounter various trials, knowing that the testing of your faith produces perseverance."

Similarly, nineteenth-century evangelist George Müller said, "To learn strong faith is to endure great trials."[43] Trials are a part of life. The caterpillar emerges as a butterfly through the struggle of exiting the cocoon. Trials are necessary to grow our faith and are not easy to endure. In fact, some are so great that we cannot endure them unless God intervenes. Thankfully, God does.

As the saying goes, "If it was easy, everybody would be doing it." We are not called to ease but to endurance in our God-given pursuits. Faith grows when we have to dig deep to reach our holy ambitions. Jesus suffered the agony of the cross for the joy of making a way for humanity to be reconciled to God. We must suffer through the hardship and setbacks for the joy of reaching our God-given goals.

WORSHIP

Psalms 95:8 joyfully says, "Come let us worship and bow down; let us kneel before the Lord our God our Maker!"

Worship is the act of expressing love and reverence to God. It should be done privately in the believer's life and publicly as God's people gather in the church.

---

43 https://www.georgemuller.org/quotes/category/trials/2

Private Worship

Private worship includes personal times of encounter with God. This can occur while we are engaged in spiritual disciplines, like being on our knees in the "prayer closet," pouring our heart out to God, or studying with an open Bible. Or it can be engaged in during more common activities like while taking a walk in the woods or driving in the car. The location of private worship is not that important; the encounter with God is what builds faith.

My friend Wayne was in a men's Bible study at the church I pastored. One night, while driving home from work, he had an encounter with God while driving in his truck. He wasn't expecting it, but he was so overcome by the presence of God that he started crying and praying. He had to pull his truck over to the side of the road. Wayne changed that night! His faith grew. He became more God-centered and hungry to do and be more for God. Worship grows faith!

Public Worship

Public worship is also a means God uses to grow our faith. When we gather together with other believers, we are strengthened by seeing others who believe as we do. There is faith-building power in the forms of public worship: singing songs, public prayers, the proclamation of the Scripture, giving an offering, taking communion together, seeing new believers baptized, and seeing people from all walks of life make public commitments to a deeper walk with God. That is why we are admonished, "Forsake not the assembling of ourselves together" (Hebrews 10:25). I can think of many times I did not "feel" like going to church but went anyway. When the service was over, I was glad I went, and my faith was refreshed.

Obedient Living

According to John 14:21, "He who has my commandments and keeps them, he it is who loves me. And he who loves me shall be loved by my Father, and I will love him and manifest myself to him."

Faith and obedience are two sides of the same coin. When we live by the commands of the Bible, our understanding of God grows deeper, and our faith grows stronger. Acting on our beliefs solidifies the "rightness" of the choices we make. The German pastor and theologian Dietrich Bonhoeffer said, "Only he who believes is obedient, and only he who is obedient believes."[44]

Obedience *does not* save us from sin; Jesus did the work of salvation on the cross. Nor does God love us because we are obedient. God is love and is not conditioned by what we do. Simply, obedience shows our love for God. Following Jesus shows how much we love him, not the other way around. Obedience *does* draw us closer to God in understanding. When we love and understand God better, our faith in him grows.

CONCLUSION

Devoted, developed, and directed faith, be it as "small as a mustard seed," can move mountains. When we put into practice the concepts of this chapter, faith will grow. In the next chapter, we will see the foundation of all faith: faith in *Christ* for life and life eternal.

---

44 https://bibleportal.com/bible-quote/belief-obedience-only-he-who-believes-is-obedient-and-only-he-who-is-obedient-believes

CAN DO; GO DO

- ◊ Look over the faith-growing principles. Can you think of a time when God used one of these ways to grow your faith?
- ◊ Commit to spending more time engaging with God through the study of the Bible.

CHAPTER 11
SALVATION VACATION

Faith in Jesus is the foundation for reaching our God-given potential.

"For the Lord is willing that none should perish, but all would come to repentance."

2 PETER 3:9

"Jesus not only saved my soul but my life as well."

BOB HOGGARD

My friend Bob and I would often go out on Sunday afternoons and visit new people who attended our morning church service. Over the years, we had the privilege of sharing with people the good news of salvation through repentance from sin and faith in Christ. I also had the privilege of getting to know Bob and hearing his Christian testimony.

In his younger days, Bob was like many other American men. He worked a steady job, was married, and had two children. Every year, he and the family would load up the car and drive down to Florida for a couple of weeks of vacation. At this time in his life, he wasn't much of a churchgoer. He wasn't mad at God, but God was not his priority.

One year, as the family drove into Daytona Beach, Bob was not feeling well. He asked his son to drive to the hotel so Bob could get some rest in the back seat. Bob pulled the car into a parking lot, crawled into the back of the station wagon, and had a massive heart attack! It just so happened that the parking lot he pulled into belonged to a hospital. They were able to get Bob to the emergency room where a medical worker saved his life. Bob spent the next couple of months trying to recover from the coronary.

As the days turned into weeks, Bob's wife, Onella, befriended one of the nurses in the hospital, who gave her a Gideon Bible. Onella began to read Scripture and pray for her husband. Bob started to get better.

As Bob's condition improved and he became stronger, he was visited by a pastor. The two became friends, and the pastor told Bob about what it meant to have a personal relationship with God. Bob heard the life-changing message of how Jesus died on the cross for the sins of the world and rose from the dead to prove that everything he said was true. The pastor asked Bob if he would like to know Jesus, and Bob said yes. Bob bowed his head and called on Jesus to save him. Jesus became the Lord of his life.

Bob said, "The change was immediate. Before I left the hospital, I stopped smoking, drinking, and started tithing!" Bob understood that turning from sin was a small price to pay for so great a salvation. After his conversion to Christ, Bob became active in sharing his faith with others. He wanted lost people to know there is a Savior who loves them. As Bob developed and matured in his faith, he served God in all sorts of ministry and leadership positions in the local church.

The starting point of success is not to seek success but to seek Jesus. To call him "Lord" means he is to be first place in all we believe and do. To seek success without the Savior is a futile pursuit; it cannot satisfy. As revivalist preacher Jonathan Edwards said, "The enjoyment of God is the only happiness with which our souls can be satisfied."[45]

---

45 https://www.ccel.org/ccel/edwards/works2.vi.xvi.ii.

We come to experience the love of God in a soul-saving and life-transforming way when we place our faith in Jesus Christ as Savior and Lord. This essential message of God's grace in salvation is that through believing in the crucifixion and resurrection of Christ to forgive us our sins against God, Jesus will save us for all eternity. It is a free gift—not because of what we do but because of what Jesus has done on the cross. We can come into a personal relationship with God when we understand and believe the following truth.

God Loves Us and Created Us to Know Him

The famous verse John 3:16 tells us, "For God so loved the world that He gave his only begotten Son, that whosoever believes in him will not perish, but have everlasting life."

People seek love, fulfillment, success, and significance. These needs and desires are not wrong in themselves, but achieving them cannot make us right with God. Jesus asked a question that probes much deeper than earthly concerns: "What shall it profit a man if he gains the whole world and loses his own soul?" (Mark 8:36). Our greatest need, the only one that ultimately matters, is to know God and live in peace with him.

Have you ever looked up at the sky on a clear night? As we look at the moon and stars and contemplate the vastness of the universe, it is amazing to think the Creator would love us and want us to know him. Due to our lack of true knowledge when it comes to God, we would understand if he were to ignore us or not care about us. We might think he has more important things to do than be concerned about us. Not true! Humans are not irrelevant to the Lord.

Jesus said, "I came that you might have life and have it in

abundance" (John 10:10). God is a good God and always wants the best for his creation. The problem is never with God. It is with us. Our sin keeps us from realizing that God created us, loves us, and wants us to know him.

PEOPLE ARE SINFUL AND SEPARATED FROM GOD; THAT IS WHY THEY HAVE NOT EXPERIENCED HIS LOVE AND PLAN FOR THEIR LIVES

Romans 3:23 says, "For all have sinned and fall short of the glory of God." Isaiah 59: 1–2 likewise explains, "Behold, the Lord's hand is not shortened, that it cannot save; neither his ear heavy, that it cannot hear: But your iniquities have come between you and your God, and your sins have hid his face from you, that he will not hear."

People are created in the image of God. We have value and worth. This is why we can create skyscrapers, write poetry, make music and art, build ships that cross the skies and oceans, develop computers, heal the sick, and show compassion to each other. God has made us with great potential for good.

Even so, the world is marred and stained. We would have to agree it is fundamentally flawed: murder, crime, addiction, theft, hate, unforgiveness, deception, discontent, and inequity seem to run rampant. We do things we know are wrong and don't do things we know are right. We know better but don't do better. We may believe that a "god" exists, but we largely ignore him. The word the Bible uses to describe this condition is "sin."

People are sinners by nature and by choice. There is something within us that wants to rebel. If the speed limit on the road is fifty-five miles per hour, we want to go faster. A stop sign really means "Slow down and only stop if you see a car coming." We are all under the downward drag of sin. We so often fight the impulse to do wrong instead of naturally doing right. Would we not all agree, if we are being honest, that we do not love God with all our heart, soul, and might, or our neighbor as ourselves?

All sin is ultimately against God. As a result, our natural state or condition is to be separated from him, both presently and eternally. Sin keeps us from knowing him in a true and saving way and causes us to suffer his wrath. In order to know God and be saved from condemnation, we have to receive the remedy for sin.

Some believe the remedy for sin is to do more good things than bad and thus earn favor with God. In this scenario, if someone's "good" outweighs their "bad," they believe God will treat them well and let them go to heaven when they die. So they work hard and try to be nice to people and volunteer and give money to charity in order to feel good about themselves and show their "goodness."

The problem with believing in one's own goodness is that it fails to ask the fundamental question: who decides what is good enough? No one lives, gives, or serves as much as they should. No one is truly doing all they can do to be as good as they can be. Some do better than others, but everyone would likely agree we could do more.

A second problem with thinking that goodness will make us right with God is that our standard of good is lower than God's standard of good. God's standard of good is perfect obedience to his law as written in the Bible. (No one other than Jesus is perfect). The apostle James put it this way: "For whosoever shall keep the whole Law, and yet disobey it in just one point, he is guilty of all" (James 2:10). Ninety-nine-percent obedience is not good enough to pass God's righteousness test!

Consider this: suppose we were in North America, given a bow and arrow, and asked to hit the exact center of a target located in Africa. We could stand on the shores of the Atlantic

Ocean and let our arrows fly. Some arrows would go farther than others, but no arrow would make it to the other side and hit the target. Why? Because no human is good enough to shoot an arrow that far, much less hit a target!

Or suppose we were all standing on the shores of the Atlantic and had to swim across the ocean to Europe. Some would jump into the water and immediately get out because the water is too cold. Some would start the journey but not make it over the breakers. Others would be eaten by sharks. If the heartiest among us could swim for ten, twenty, fifty, or one hundred miles, they would still not make it because it is not humanly possible to swim from the United States to Europe. No one is good enough to do it.

The same is true with trying to be good enough to be accepted by God on our own. Some are "better" than others, but none are good enough to win God's approval.

Of all the people I have spoken to about Christ, all agreed (except one, but he had genuine mental issues) they had sinned at least once. They usually rationalized by saying, "Everyone sins, so it's no big deal." But it is a big deal: "For the wages of sin is death" (Romans 6:23).

What we earn for sinning is eternal separation from God in a place called hell. We don't want that, and God doesn't want that for us. Thankfully, Jesus has made a better way. What is the way?

JESUS DIED AND ROSE AGAIN TO SAVE US FROM OUR SIN

Paul wrote the Romans, "God demonstrated his own love toward us in that when we were still sinners, Christ died for us" (Romans 5:8).

And 1 Peter 3:8 tells Christians, "Christ died for our sins, the just for the unjust, so that he might bring us to God, having been put to death in the flesh and made alive in the Spirit."

God is love, and he is also just. Because he is perfectly just, he must punish the injustice of sin. God knew the cost of sin was greater than our ability to pay. Because God is love, he provided a way to escape the condemning consequences of sin: he sent Jesus, who died on the cross as a sacrifice for sin and payment for the penalty sin incurs. That's the good news! Mankind's greatest problem, sin, has been paid by Christ's death on the cross. As Romans 6:23, also mentioned in the previous section, continues on to say, "For the wages of sin is death, *but the free gift of God is eternal life in Jesus Christ* (emphasis added).

Salvation is not a reward for being good; it is a gift God gives to us based on the goodness of Jesus.

To be "saved" by Christ means to be rescued and delivered from the penalty and punishment of sin. It means we can be forgiven and cleansed. Isaiah 53:6 explains, "All of us like sheep have gone astray. Each of us has turned to his own way. But the Lord has caused the iniquity of us all to fall upon him [Jesus]."

In the Old Testament, the Israelite priest would offer on an altar the sacrifice of a lamb without defect. The animal would atone for—or "cover over"—the sins of the people. The shed blood of the unblemished lamb would serve as a temporary substitute for the sinful people. Peter admonished his audience, "You were not redeemed from your forefathers' empty way of life with perishable things like gold or silver, but with the precious blood of Christ, a lamb without blemish or defect" (1 Peter 1:18–19).

Jesus died in our place as a permanent *substitute* for us and final payment for the accumulated sins of the world. His death covered the sin bill you and I could never do enough good works to repay. His sacrifice makes all other sacrifices for sin unneeded.

Jesus is the only one who can make us right with God. No

major religious figure in history ever claimed to die for the sins of the world. Nor was anyone ever good enough to qualify as worthy to commit such a sacrificial act. Jesus, the sinless Son of God, is the only one who makes the claim and meets the criteria. Not only did Jesus die for our sins, but he also rose from the dead to prove he has power over death and that all he said is true. This is why Jesus said with authority, "I am the way, the truth, and the life. No one comes to the Father, but by me" (John 14:6).

WE MUST PLACE OUR FAITH IN CHRIST AND RECEIVE HIM AS SAVIOR AND LORD

Galatians 2:16 declares, "Knowing that a man is not justified by the works of the law, but by the faith of Jesus Christ, *even we have believed in Jesus Christ*, that we might be justified by the faith of Christ, and not by the works of the law: for by the works of the law shall no flesh be justified" (emphasis added).

John 1:12 says, "But as many as received him, to them he gave the right to become the children of God, even to those that believe on his name."

Romans similarly promises, "That if you confess with your mouth the Lord Jesus and believe in your heart God has raised him from the dead, you shall be saved" (Romans 10:9).

Becoming a Christian requires something to believe and someone to receive. We must believe the good news that God has provided salvation through Jesus. We must also personally receive Jesus as Lord and Savior.

Salvation is a free gift. We cannot earn it, nor do we deserve it. As all gifts, salvation must be received. If someone offers a valuable gift to us, it is disrespectful not to receive it gladly. That would be "snubbing" the giver. To receive Christ means we trust him to come into our heart when we place our faith in his death and resurrection to save us from our sin and make us right with God.

Think of marriage. A woman wants to marry the man she loves. She has seen others get married and wants it for herself. She believes she should get married. She has even read books about marriage. But she is not married until, forsaking all others, she commits to the man she loves and says, "I do." She receives him as her husband. That's the difference between knowing about a wedding and getting married.

Salvation presents a similar picture: Someone can have an understanding of what it means to receive Jesus as Savior and Lord but not make the commitment to receive him as Lord of their heart and life. They know they should and believe they eventually will, but not yet. For faith to be genuine, the commitment must be made.

PRAYER OF FAITH

Have you made the life-changing commitment of receiving Jesus by placing your faith in him? Have you said "I do" to receiving Jesus as your Savior and Lord? If not, you can do so right now. Consider the following questions:

- ⋄ Do you believe God loves you and created you to know him?

- ⋄ Do you believe your sin has separated you from God?

- ⋄ Do you believe Jesus died and rose again to pay the penalty for your sin?

- ⋄ Are you sorry about your sinful condition and ready to turn to Jesus for forgiveness?

If the heartfelt answer to these questions is yes, then call out to Jesus, and he will save. The following is a suggested prayer to help. The words themselves are not magic but are an expression of faith and what you believe in your heart.

> Lord Jesus, I need you. I realize my sin has separated me from God, and I am sorry. I ask forgiveness. I believe you died on the cross for my sin and rose from the dead to pardon me. I turn from my sin and call upon you to forgive my sin. I receive you as my Savior and Lord. I accept your free gift of eternal life. Make me the kind of person you want me to be. Amen.

The starting point of a can-do attitude is to believe in Jesus! No Jesus, no success—even if we achieve everything in this world for which we strive.

Knowing Jesus is success—in this life as well as the life to come.

CHAPTER 12
DRUNK MONKEYS

We must cultivate and develop a God-given faith in our talents and abilities to reach our God-given potential.

"And what shall we say to these things, if God be for us, who can be against us."

ROMANS 8:31

"You are an unstoppable force who develops your craft, serves your clients well and never gives up!"

STEVEN EDWARDS

My first semester of seminary was a struggle. In college, I was an okay student and did what I needed to do to make okay grades and get by. But seminary was different because I was studying something that I planned to devote my life to. I was preparing for the ministry.

I put in a lot more hours studying the Bible and theology. I would get up in the morning, take my wife to work, take classes in the morning, and go to the library in the afternoon. Late afternoon, I would pick up my wife. We would have dinner, and then I would study more. But the effort I was expending did not translate into higher grades.

I was frustrated. I believed God wanted me in seminary and

wanted me to do well, and I thought I had a good grasp of what I was learning, but it was not coming through on test grades. This led to less confidence in my ability. Frustration and lower confidence is not a formula for maximizing results. What did I need to do to get the result I was seeking?

One night, while writing a term paper, I was praying and thinking about my situation. I told the Lord I believed he'd called me to ministry and seminary, but I was frustrated over my subpar performance. I was in the place I wanted to be, doing what I thought God wanted me to do, working harder at it than anything I had worked at in the past. Though I would have liked to see better results, I was committed to seeing it through.

It was then I believe God put a verse in my head and heart: "What shall we say to these things, if God be for us, who can be against us" (Romans 8:31). I had studied Romans 8:31–39 and preached from the text. Now God gave grace to apply the principle to my situation! I believed he was for me, not against me, in my academic pursuits.

This understanding gave me a newfound confidence in my learning. I wasn't any smarter or more hardworking than I was a minute before. The only difference was that I believed better. I believed God called me to seminary, gave me a mind to comprehend his truth, wanted me to succeed, and was helping me do it.

My attitude toward school changed in several ways. One, I believed God would help me to achieve academically. I did not have to struggle under my own power; I could depend on his. I stopped wishing for better grades and trusted him for them. For the next two years, I was on the dean's list and made straight As.

Second, my stress levels went down. I stopped worrying about every question that could be asked on a test. I stopped being so anxious and preoccupied with questions such as "Am I studying enough? Do I know all of this?" I realized that if I worked hard and prepared, I could trust God to provide.

Third, I stopped looking at school as a competition between classmates. Before, I thought I needed to outperform other students because there were only so many As for the class. After, I realized I needed to be the best student God called me to be, and that if there was an A to be had, he would give it to me. If he wanted other students to get an A, he could do that as well. This "win-win" disposition freed me to pray for my classmates to do well. I wanted them to succeed, as God did.

GOD WANTS US TO THINK BETTER

Self-doubt, low self-esteem, an inferiority complex, insecurity, feelings of inadequacy, or any other thoughts or feelings that lead to limiting beliefs are planted in the mind by the deceiver and not God. The devil is a master at putting doubt and despair in our heads: "You're not good enough," "It will never work," "What makes you so special?" "You'll only embarrass yourself." We have to push back! We may not be able to completely vanquish the thoughts, but we don't have to believe them. We can push through to the glory of God!

All the tools, talent, skills, opportunities, and resources at our disposal will not cause us to reach our maximum potential if we don't believe God is for us and can do it through us. Remember, God is not limited by our lack of faith. He can still do anything he wants. He is sovereign and omnipotent. But lack of faith limits us. Sometimes we do not see the hand of God because we will not trust him. We have to believe our goal is possible! A person will generally not do better until they believe better of themselves and God. Start believing, and go to work on mastering your skills.

Some people think believing in oneself is prideful. It is true that "we should not think more highly of ourselves than we ought." It is also true that we should not think less of ourselves than God made us to be. He has given us gifts, talents, opportunities, and blessings. We should not brag about them and think that because of them we are superior to other people. We should accept them, maximize them, and believe he wants us to use them for his glory and the good of others.

Hoosiers is a movie about a small-town high school basketball team from Indiana that makes it to the state championship and wins. On their way to winning it all, they face many tough opponents. In the regional final, the team is down by a few points with less than three minutes to go. The coach calls a time-out to give his young players instructions.

As the team goes back onto the floor, one of the players, Strap Purl, bows down on the sideline in prayer.

Coach Norman implores him, "Let's go, Strap," but Strap doesn't budge from his prayer of supplication.

The coach leans over and calmly says to his timid player, "Strap, God wants you on the floor."

Coach Norman's words of assurance make all the difference in the world. Strap rises from prayer with a confident smile on his face. He runs out on the floor and quickly scores four points to give his team the lead. Cheerleaders are rooting frantically as the gym erupts with loud applause.

Coach Norman calls another time-out. As Strap comes back to the bench, Coach asks Strap, "What got into you?"

Strap replies with a courageous expression, "The Lord. I can feel his strength."

What changed in Strap? What caused a timid athlete to dominate at a crucial moment when the game was on the line? What changed was the belief that he could make a difference because God was for him! Strap believed he could score by God's power. This fictional story tells a powerful truth: believing God is for us can make an incredible difference in our confidence and faith.

We may not have a human coach whispering words of affirmation in our ears, but we have the Holy Spirit speaking words of encouragement to our hearts: "I am with you," "You can do it," "All things are possible to him who believes." All are words of affirmation God speaks to his children.

HOW TO THINK BETTER

Jesus was asked by an expert in the law, "Which is the greatest commandment?" He responded by quoting from the Old Testament book of Deuteronomy 6:5: "You shall love the Lord your God with all your heart, with all your soul, with all your mind, and with all your strength" (Mark 12:30). This means people are to love God with the totality of their person, firstly and completely. We are to love God with all that we are because of the greatness of all he is.

This includes our thoughts. God has given us a mind. With it, we choose to think—either good or bad. As Proverbs 23:7 puts it, "As a man thinks in his heart, so is he."

Thoughts, understanding, belief, awareness, decision-making, and other parts of our psychological makeup are products of the mind and heart. If we want to believe better, we must think better.

We have probably all heard Christians refer to themselves as "sinners saved by grace." The emphasis is usually on the word "sinners." This is true, but it is not a complete picture of a believer in Christ. When the gift of salvation is received by the repentant sinner, the Bible says, "God has delivered us from the domain of darkness and transferred us to the kingdom of his beloved Son" (Colossians 1:13). We are more than sinners saved by grace. We are saints of God and members of God's family (Ephesians 2:19).

Believers live in a new reality with a mind that is being renewed. Our thoughts reflect the new realm in which we operate; we think of love, faith, hope, joy, peace, gratitude, humility, victory, and success God's way, to name a few.

We have been given access, through Scripture and the enlightenment of the Holy Spirit, to understand the ways of God. These thoughts must be planted in the mind and heart and nourished in order to take root. The following principles can help us develop a better understanding of how we should think better of ourselves.

Cultivate the Mind of Christ

Every Christian has something greater than human wisdom; they have the mind of Christ (1 Corinthians 2:16). Having the mind of Christ means we are able to see the world from God's point of view. It also means we have the ability to live a life that is pleasing and obedient to God through the power of the Holy Spirit directing our thoughts and actions. It does not mean we will know everything God knows, but it does mean our minds and hearts are able to receive all that God wants us to know in this life.

The mind of Christ is *given* to every believer when they place their faith in Christ as Savior and Lord. It is one of the many gifts of salvation. We *cultivate* the mind of Christ through devotion to him in developing Christian disciplines, such as studying the Bible, prayer, worship, fellowship, giving, service, and developing the fruit of the Spirit in our hearts and lives.

Knowing that we have the mind of Christ should give us a belief boost. We can be confident that God is already committed to helping us think better. In addition, Christ is feeding into our mind his thoughts and plans for us.

Cooperate with the Holy Spirit

"Do not quench the Spirit," warns 1 Thessalonians 5:19.

From the moment we are saved, the Holy Spirit of God begins to work in us to mature us and make us more like Christ. We have to allow him to do his work and cooperate with him by listening to his voice and obeying Scripture. When we mentally say and think, *No* to the Spirit, we are quenching his work and not cooperating with God to renew our mind.

What is the best way to cooperate with the Holy Spirit? Stop arguing and start agreeing with him.

When my son was small, we were at the store buying groceries. It was getting late and close to his bedtime. As I put the food on the conveyer belt at the cash register, he saw a piece of candy he "had" to have and asked me to get it for him. I said no. It was too close to his bedtime, and I did not want to start a habit of buying him candy every time we went to the store. He threw a fit—a Chernobyl meltdown in the checkout line at Food Lion! He argued, cried, and reached for the candy. He was very uncooperative. The only thing I could say to him was "We are going to have a talk when we get home." "Talk" was code for a more severe punishment.

When it comes to God, I can be a lot like my son wanting candy. I want what I want when I want it. I want to argue and resist the Spirit. I wish to be guided by carnal impulses instead of a renewed mind.

Don't live in the grip of such a mentality. Say yes to God immediately! Everything God tells us to do is for his glory and will work for our good. The key is to cooperate as he transforms our hearts and minds by Christ Jesus.

Change Our Thoughts

There is a battle going on *in* our mind and *for* our mind (2 Corinthians 10:4–5). We live in a fallen world that is opposed to God and wants us to adopt a self-defeating mindset. We also struggle with temptations and sinful thoughts that are detrimental to a godly life and that of a successful Christian witness. In addition, the devil attempts to deceive us through wrong thoughts he plants in our mind.

Thankfully, we don't have to listen to the world, the flesh, or the devil. By the grace of God, we have the ability to "take every thought captive in obedience to Christ" (2 Corinthians 10:5). We may not be able to control every thought that pops into our heads, but we can decide whether or not to entertain them. We can decide what to think about our thoughts. Change your thoughts, and change your life.

How do we change our thoughts? One way is by realizing we can! After all, as 1 John 4:4 says, "Greater is he that is in me than he that is in the world."

We don't have to listen to the goofy thoughts that pop into our heads. Think of the mind as a radio. If we don't like what we are hearing, we can change the channel. Ask God to give you honest, uplifting, lovely thoughts you can tune in to, and dial into them.

A second way we can change our thoughts is by changing what we put in our minds. Remember the old computer saying: "Garbage in, garbage out." What are we reading? What are we watching? What are we listening to? What preoccupies our thoughts? These questions are important because they influence the way we think, positively and negatively. We have to get the garbage out and put the good stuff in.

As he did with the Ephesians, the apostle Paul likens the Christian experience to taking off dirty clothes and putting on new, clean clothes in his letters to the Colossians: "You have put off the old self with its practices and have put on the new self, which is being renewed in knowledge after the image of its creator" (Colossians 3:9–10 ESV). This principle applies to the way we live and also how we think. If we don't think right, we won't be right or act right.

Put Off the Old Self

Putting off the old self equates to getting the detrimental moral and mental garbage out of our lives. Think of the vehicles that sometimes drive our thinking: television, radio, movies, videos, computers, cell phones, podcasts, social media—all of them competing for our attention and attempting to influence our attitude and thinking. They can take us down mental roads that lead to a dead end or off a cliff.

According to digitalmarketing.org, 3.96 billion people use social media—almost half of the world's population! Global internet users spend 144 minutes on social media sites every day. Americans spend two hours and three minutes per day on social media. On average, people swipe, type, click, or tap their phone 2,617 times a day. For heavy users, the number jumps to 5,427 times per day.[46] We seem to live in a world that is addicted to electronic devices.

Media devices are neither good nor bad. What determines their effect on us is how we use them and, I think, how often we use them. If we use them to troll others, watch inappropriate material, listen to gossip, or spread hate, we are putting in garbage. If we are wasting endless hours of time online instead of doing something productive, we are putting in garbage. Put off the old self!

Put on the New Self

New and improved is how we should see ourselves. We have

---

46 https://www.digitalmarketing.org/blog/how-much-time-does-the-average-person-spend-on-social-media

been made new through the cross of Christ and must fill our minds with the good things of God. Paul told the Philippians, "Finally my brethren, whatever is true, whatever is honorable, whatever is just, whatever is pure, whatever is lovely, whatever is commendable, if there is any excellence, if there is anything worthy of praise, *think* about these things" (Philippians 4:8, emphasis added).

My wife and I once bought a brand-new car. It was cleaner and shinier than any vehicle we had ever owned. It looked new, smelled new, and had no miles on the motor. I wanted to keep it that way. In the same way, as Dr. Adrian Rogers explained earlier, we should want to keep the "new self" fresh. We do this through filling our mind with Scripture, solid preaching, uplifting music, great books, positive media, stimulating conversations, articles that sharpen our intellect, and other things that encourage us to walk with God and live for his glory and the good of others.

Choose Who Influences Us

Who we hang around can have much to do with who we become. Business philosopher Jim Rohn said, "You are the average of the five people you spend the most time with."[47] The story of the "Stranglers and Wranglers" will illustrate the point.[48]

Many years ago at the University of Wisconsin, a group of talented male writers got together to evaluate each other's writings. Each would read his prose out loud, and the others would take turns dissecting and criticizing what had been written. So brutal were their evaluations that they called themselves the "stranglers."

At the same time, a group of women writers from the same school got together to evaluate each other's writing. Instead of

---

47 https://institutesuccess.com/library/you-are-the-average-of-the-five-people-you-spend-the-most-time-with-jim-rohn-2/
48 https://alltimeshortstories.com/wranglers-and-stranglers

criticizing each other, they determined to encourage each other and offer suggestions to help the writer improve. They were known as the "wranglers."

Twenty years later, some interesting results came to light. Not one member of the "stranglers" achieved any literary success. By contrast, several members of the "wranglers" attained literary significance. Included in the group was Marjorie K. Rawlings, who won a Pulitzer Prize for *The Yearling*.

These were two groups of people who had much potential and talent. What made the difference? A key factor was that one group chose to lift each other up while the other chose to tear each other down. The "wranglers" believed in each other. The "stranglers" belittled each other.

Make friends with people who will encourage you and challenge you to become better. Associate with people who build you up and don't tear you down. Look for people who live out the fruit of the Spirit of love, joy, peace, patience, goodness, kindness, gentleness, faithfulness, and self-control. They will bring blessings to your life.

Counter Negative Self-Talk with Scriptural Affirmations

Some solid advice is to "talk to yourself more than you listen to yourself." What do you say when you talk to yourself? This internal monologue of the mind is known as "self-talk." Thousands of thoughts come into our heads every day. Our minds tend to listen to worry and doubt, run toward the negative, and quench the voice of the Holy Spirit. It is easier to talk ourselves out of doing something that requires faith than to talk ourselves into it.

To counter the destructive self-talk, scriptural affirmations can be used to build faith. Scriptural affirmations are biblical statements that tell us who God is and who we are in Christ. We can use them to train our minds toward God and build our faith. When we repeat them, we remind ourselves of the power of God when our faith needs bolstering.

Scriptural affirmation is *not* a magic mantra that will cause something to happen if we say it often enough. It is not a "name it and claim it" recipe to manipulate the hand of God into getting whatever we want. Instead, it is a powerful way to "set your mind on things above where Christ is seated at the right hand of God" (Colossians 3:2). It is a way of reminding ourselves of the "all things" freely given to us in Christ (Romans 8:32). Don't put your faith in the affirmation. Use the affirmation to have stronger faith in Christ.

The following are twenty faith-building scriptural affirmations. Use them along with other Scripture to build your trust in God and believe him for greater things in Christ.

- ⋄ God is in control. (Isaiah 14:24)
- ⋄ The Lord is my shepherd. (Psalms 23:1)
- ⋄ The Lord is my helper. (Hebrews 13:6)
- ⋄ Jesus is Lord. (Romans 10:9)
- ⋄ I can do all things through Christ who strengthens me. (Philippians 4:13)
- ⋄ With God all things are possible. (Matthew 19:26)
- ⋄ Greater is he that is in me than he that is in the world. (1 John 4:4)
- ⋄ I am loved by God. (Romans 5:8)
- ⋄ I am a child of God. (John 1:12)
- ⋄ God wants me to do well. (3 John 1:2)

- God wants me to succeed in his plans for me. (Jeremiah 29:11)
- God is for me. (Romans 8:31)
- I am more than a conqueror through Christ. (Romans 8:37)
- I am forgiven. (Ephesians 4:32)
- I am saved. (Romans 10:10)
- I am the head and not the tail. (Deuteronomy 28:13)
- By my God I can jump a wall. (Psalms 18:29)
- God can do exceedingly and abundantly beyond all I can hope or imagine. (Ephesians 3:20)
- I am strong in God. (Joel 3:10)
- The same power that raised Christ from the dead works in me. (Ephesians 1:19)
- Nothing is impossible with God. (Luke 1:37)

How to Use Scriptural Affirmations

1. *Repeat the affirmation or Bible verse out loud*: When we do this, we engage the mind, mouth, and ears. Cognitive science tells us that the more sensory methods we use in learning, the more apt something is to stick.

2. *Repeat the affirmation many times, slowly, emphasizing each word of the statement or verse*: It may take repeating the statement a few times to get our minds and hearts engaged. Don't burn through it and say, "This doesn't work." Stick with it until the spiritual cobwebs clear.

3. *Think about each word being said*: There is no magic in repeating words. Faith comes when we believe that the words apply to us. Before he was king of Israel, David was a shepherd boy. He spent many days and nights tending sheep and thinking about God. While out on the hills and pastures, he probably had lots of time to think about God, sheep, and shepherds. As he thought, he came to a life-changing truth: "The Lord is *my* Shepherd" (Psalms 23:1). Scriptural affirmations are faith-building, life-changing truth.

4. *Say it with emotion until it sinks in*: Use excited voice inflection to emphasize the words. Anticipate how God will bring about what you are saying. Raise your hand in the air and pump your fist. It may feel awkward, but it works! When we tie the words to an emotional anchor, the belief becomes stronger.

King David did not sing psalms in monotone. The words came from the depths of a heart devoted to God. When David brought the ark of the covenant into Jerusalem, he danced before the Lord. David's faith was great because he was not afraid to say it loud and proud when he talked about God's goodness toward him.

DON'T LISTEN TO DRUNK MONKEYS

Steven Edwards has been in real estate for over thirty years. He began as a real estate agent when interest rates for home mortgages were in the double digits. Over time, he became very successful, personally selling over a thousand homes. In 2003, he and some other associates opened the Real Estate Group in Chesapeake, Virginia. The brokerage quickly became the number-one-producing real estate office in Hampton Roads, Virginia. In 2009, a second office was opened in Virginia Beach, Virginia. It has become the second-highest-producing real estate office in Hampton Roads. Agents working out of the two locations help thousands of clients find great homes year in and year out.

To educate and motivate real estate agents to thrive in the profession, Steven introduced a series of classes. These classes deal with both the nuts and bolts of selling real estate as well as the mindset of a successful agent. In one of the lessons, he communicates the importance of fostering positive self-talk and not listening to negative self-talk. In order to illustrate the point, he brings out the "drunk monkey." It is a stuffed animal with inebriated eyes and a cloth bottle of liquor sewn onto his hand. Steven sits the monkey on his shoulder and repeats what the drunk monkey might say: "You're no good," "You can't sell real estate," "You're an imposter," or "You're a loser." He then goes on to caution the agents about listening to negative self-talk.

The "drunk monkey" is not exclusive to selling real estate. He can sit on anyone's shoulder, filling our minds with negative self-talk. Don't listen to him. Replace his loathing phrases toward you with loving phrases from God.

JESUS WANTS US TO THINK BETTER AND BELIEVE BETTER

During Jesus's earthly ministry, he performed many miracles. He calmed a raging sea, walked on water, cast out demons, healed the sick, and brought the dead back to life. He is quite a miracle worker.

On one occasion, after an extended season of ministering in the region of Galilee, Jesus returned with his disciples to his hometown of Nazareth. As was his custom, he went to the synagogue to teach. But people were offended by his speaking the Word of God. To them, Jesus was nothing special. He was just the son of Mary and a carpenter. He was not worthy of honor. Sadly, they did not believe in his message of salvation or his healing ministry. As a result, "he could do no mighty work there, except to lay hands on a few sick folk and heal them" (Mark 6:5).

How sad for the unbelieving people. Jesus could and would do works among them, but they would not have it. Commenting on this occasion in his study Bible, pastor John MacArthur tells us, "He [Jesus] had the power to do more miracles, but not the will, because they rejected him. Miracles belonged among those who were ready to believe."[49]

I may not understand all of the ramifications about my faith and God's power. His power is certainly not limited by my lack of faith. He is omnipotent and can do whatever he wants. Nor does my faith obligate him to provide whatever I want; because he is omniscient, he knows what is truly best for me. Yet my believing and God's working do intertwine. I liken it to being a weak string woven into a massive rope. By myself, I am easily broken, but sewn into the fabric of God's power, I am unstoppable. And so are you.

We don't have to have perfect faith or absolute assurance in pursuing our God-given dreams and goals, but we do have to have the faith of a mustard seed, as small as it is, to see God move mountains. Don't let your "I can't" keep you from God's "I can." Miracles belong to those who are ready to believe!

---

[49] The MacArthur Study Bible, English Standard Version (Wheaton, Ill.: Crossway, 2010) 1434, note on Mark 6:5.

CONCLUSION

God thinks highly of us as children of God through faith in Christ. We must think better of ourselves! We are not defeated and defenseless. We have the power of God working in us and through us. If we adopt the mindset of a child of God and develop the methods of thinking his thoughts toward us, we can do all things through Christ who strengthens us!

CAN DO; GO DO

- ◇ Look over the section "How to Think Better" and focus on each one.
- ◇ Follow the formula and repeat the scriptural affirmations. Return to them daily until they sink in.

SECTION 4

"DO"

Achieving our God-given goals and dreams requires constant action and perseverance.

"I can **do** all things through Christ who strengthens me."

CHAPTER 13
LIGHTS, CAMERA, ACTION: TAKE ACTION AND START DOING

"Faith without works is dead."

JAMES 2:17

"Our business is only a means to an end, and our end is to try to affect lives for eternity."

DAVID GREEN, FOUNDER OF HOBBY LOBBY

"Lights! Camera! Action!" When the director of a movie yells these words, filming is underway. Think of the preparation that has gone on behind the scenes: actors spending many hours memorizing and rehearsing their lines: stagers frantically setting up the studio with props and furniture to make the scene look authentic; members of the film crew placing each camera in the correct position, with the perfect lens and angle in order to portray the actors in the best light. All this preparation is essential but serves to support the main objective: taking action!

"God provides the wind, but man must raise the sails,"[50] said St. Augustine. How many dreams have died for lack of action?

---

50 https://www.success.com/ready-set-go-13-quotes-to-inspire-you-to-take-action

How much frustration and disappointment came from failing to take initiative to get started? How many of us, myself included, have let inactivity win because we listened to the voices in our heads telling us, "Not now," "You can't," "It's too hard," "You will fail." Failure to take action is the only guaranteed failure.

GOD ACTS!

Jeremiah 32:17 declares, "Ah Lord God! Behold, you have made the heavens and the earth by your great power and outstretched arm! Nothing is too difficult for you."

In every miracle of the Bible, God is acting! Consider some of the great acts of God:

- He created the world and Adam and Eve.
- He caused Sarah to become pregnant with Isaac when she was ninety years old.
- He parted the Red Sea and brought the Israelites out of Egypt.
- He caused the walls of Jericho to fall.
- He acted in the affairs of Israel.
- He raised Jesus from the dead.
- He created a people known as the church.
- He acts in changing people's lives through the gospel of Christ.
- He is active in readying the world for the second coming of Christ.

Does God act in the world today? Yes! He is still creating, sustaining, correcting, and protecting his people and his creation. He never changes. He is the same yesterday, today, and forever (Hebrews 13:8).

✦

GOD MADE US TO BE PEOPLE OF ACTION

James 1:22 encourages Christians, "But be doers of the word, and not hearers only, deceiving yourselves."

The only time the apostle Paul waited was when he waited on God to tell him what to do. He had a bent toward action, and so should we.

I heard a story about a pastor who was demonstrating to his congregation the power of taking action. He held up a one-hundred-dollar bill and asked, "Who wants a hundred dollars?" People in the congregation politely raised their hands. A few stood up and said, "I'll take it; give it to me." The pastor didn't move. Eventually, a woman ran to the front and took the money out of his hand. She got the hundred dollars. Her doing led to dollars. Benjamin Franklin became her favorite founding father.

My wife teaches high school English at an at-risk school. She considers it her dream job. It doesn't mean she likes everything about the job, but she believes she is called to it and derives satisfaction from teaching teenagers how to be better thinkers, speakers, and writers. What is so interesting is that she did not begin teaching until she was forty.

She was doing a great job raising our children and being a pastor's wife, but she believed God was calling her to more. She found out that the city we lived in had a "career switcher" program, which allowed people from other walks of life to transition into the teaching profession. She went back to Old Dominion University and earned a master of English degree. She was also accepted into the career-switcher program and placed in the public school.

Going back to school after being out of college for over fifteen years, in addition to being a wife and mother, was not easy. There were many late nights of study, reading, and preparing papers. Some of her days were spent interning in the classroom. Yet she persevered for three years until she graduated and got a job as a public high school teacher.

That was over a decade ago. Since then, she has received a master teacher certification and is faculty sponsor of the Young Life multicultural club. She is well respected in her school and known as a competent and caring educator when it comes to developing students for college and career. As I mentioned earlier, she was given the honor of Teacher of the Year for 2023. It wasn't easy, but she took action and pursued a God-given dream. By the strength of Christ in her, she was able to achieve one of her life goals!

HOW TO ACT

The following steps will help us take action to reach our full potential.

Get Clarity and Peace from God

To repeat an important verse, "For he who knows to do good and does not do it, to him it is sin" (James 4:17).

Life is a big lake of choices. If we are not careful, we will paddle endlessly, constantly changing direction until we lose energy and drown without having reached the shore of our God-given dreams. Don't drown when God is sending a lifeline of his will!

Getting clarity from God gives direction. It brings the peace of knowing the good thing God wants us to do. It becomes a lane to swim in and a path to reach the shore. (We will discuss more on determining the will of God in chapter 15). Getting clarity also narrows our choices. When we know what to do, we also know what not to do. Finally, clarity will give us confidence that we are doing the will of God and the belief that he will give us the power to reach our goals.

Make a Plan

Planning action is, in itself, an act. We don't have to have all of the details, but we need some idea of where we want to go and how to get there. Jesus wisely said, "What king, going to make war against another king, doesn't first sit down and consult whether he is able with ten thousand to meet him that comes against him with twenty thousand?" (Luke 14:31).

Great endeavors begin by asking great questions: What will it take to reach the goal? Who do I need to help me? What is the pathway for success in the endeavor? How long will it take? How much will it cost? These are great questions to ask on the front end of our pursuits. They are not questions that should stop us. They will clarify our path and prepare us for what lies ahead.

Planning and organizing are important, but don't fall prey to "paralysis of analysis." We can overthink ourselves into doubt or procrastination. Also, detailed plans have a way of needing to be changed in order to be successful. Plans should propel us *to* act, not keep us *from* acting. As Fred Factor author Mark Sanborn said, "Intention without action is only a dream. In the end, it isn't what we plan to do but what we actually do that makes a difference."[51]

---

[51] Mark Sanborn, *The Fred Factor (Colorado Springs, CO: Waterbrook Press, 2004)*.

Act Now!

There is no time to wait, because the time we wait is usually the time we waste. Act now when emotions are strong and desire is at its peak. Fulfilling our God-given dreams will take more time than we think, and there will be obstacles and detours along the way. It is natural to wait until we feel the time is right (mood) or we have more information (knowledge) or conditions are better (circumstances). But such thoughts are usually ill advised and can sabotage success. One ounce of taking action is better than a pound of thinking about it.

Don't Wait Until You "Feel" Like It

Go to work on it now, and feel the satisfaction of making progress in getting the job done. Once a plane is cleared for takeoff, it cannot sit on the runway; it has to fly. The inspiration to "do" usually comes after we have started the act of "doing" and are on our way to seeing it through to completion.

Thomas Edison invented hundreds of things: the light bulb, phonograph, movie camera, carbon microphone, mimeograph, and electric power distribution, to name a few. He did not wait to be inspired. He just kept working on a project until he got it to work.

Have a sense of urgency: time is short, and the task is worthy of starting now.

Don't Wait Until You Know It All

Mr. Edison is also quoted as saying, "The object of all work is production or accomplishment and to either of these ends there must be forethought, system, planning, intelligence, and honest purpose, as well as perspiration. Seeming to do is not doing."[52]

Retired four-star general Colin Powell used the 40-70 rule for

---

[52] https://www.edisonmuckers.org/thomas-edison-quotes/

decision-making. He believed we should not take action if we have a less than 40 percent chance of being right, but once we have 40 to 70 percent of the information needed, we should proceed. If we wait for 100 percent, we've probably waited too late.[53]

Don't Miss God's Timing

Some may think, *When I am ready, God will bless my endeavors*. It is true that we are to "wait on the Lord," but when he is telling us to move ahead, the waiting is over.

After the exodus from Egypt, God told Moses to instruct the Israelites to take possession of the land of Canaan. Moses sent twelve spies to Canaan in order to decide the best way to enter the Promised Land. The spies returned not with a plan but a "bad report." They told Moses and the people that there were giants in the land who lived in cities with fortified walls. The enemy was too big to beat. As a result, the people "lost heart" and rebelled against the Lord.

Their faith in God was overtaken by fear of moving forward. The "giants" of distraction caused the sin of inaction. The result was a forty-year delay for a journey that could have been completed in about a month. And those who were originally given the promise did not enter due to disobedience through lack of action. When God says go, the time is right.

Start Small, but Start

If you want to learn a new skill or hobby, start doing it. Buy a book, or watch a video on how to do it. Join a club that has the same interest, or, if none exist, start one. Action taken leads to more action. Keep doing it until it becomes a habit. How do we know when it's a habit? When we miss not acting on it. The smallest actions, done consistently and over time, will lead us in

---

[53] https://blog.42courses.com/home/2019/12/10/colin-powells-40-70-rule

the right direction.

Charles Spurgeon (1834–1892) was considered "the prince of preachers" in Victorian England. Though he only lived fifty-seven years, his accomplishments were prolific. He published hundreds of books, sermons, and pamphlets; pastored the Metropolitan Tabernacle for thirty-eight years; started a college for preachers as well as an orphanage for children; and preached to thousands of people every week—all of this while suffering from bouts of severe depression and gout, as well as caring for his invalid wife and raising twin boys. What was the secret to his accomplishments? According to Spurgeon, he mustered through by depending on God and doing a little every day: "The way to do a great deal is to keep on doing a little. The way to do nothing at all is to be continually resolving that you will do everything."[54]

Act with Urgency and Set a Deadline for Completion

Business runs on deadlines: the job has to get done by a certain time. Education runs on deadlines: homework is due and term papers must be submitted by a certain date. Sports run on deadlines: there is a set amount of time or a set number of attempts to beat the opponent.

Our fallen nature leads us to believe that if there is no need to move forward, then we don't have to. Wrong! Setting a deadline forces us to develop a plan for completion and complete action steps along the way. We don't have all the time in the world.

Motivational speaker W. Clement Stone used to hand out lapel pins that said, "Do it now." He would exhort his audiences to get up every morning and say, "Do it now," and repeat it fifty times.[55] Planning and organizing are important, but action is

---

54 https://www.crosswalk.com/faith/spiritual-life/inspiring-quotes/20-powerful-quotes-from-charles-spurgeon.html
55 Story told by John Maxwell, John Maxwell, *The 15 Invaluable Laws of Growth* (New York: Center Street Pub., 2012) 11.

essential. Starting can be hard, but it begins the journey of great rewards. Not starting is hard too, because not acting on what we know we should do leads to regret. Choose your hard!

Stay Focused

It is easy to get pulled in different directions that can delay action or deny us the ability to complete a task. The unexpected is a part of life; accidents do happen, circumstances can change, and crises come. Deal with them. The bigger they are, the longer it may take, but we must not let them derail us from reaching our goals.

Distraction Is De-action

Distraction is the enemy of action. How do we get distracted? We might begin thinking about how much needs to be done instead of focusing on what needs to be done next. Thinking about all of the long and difficult tasks can lead to discouragement, which makes us procrastinate or quit.

Start doing, and your thinking will produce solutions. As they say, "Inch by inch, life's a cinch; yard by yard, life is hard."

Don't Doubt; Do

"I'll never get it done" will de-motivate our good intentions. Don't make the task harder than it truly is. Doing something worthwhile may come with a learning curve and involve a lot of steps, but each step is very doable. While it may not be easy, it is not as hard as we make it out to be. We are empowered by God, and he has gifted us with the ability to do whatever he has called us to do and will empower us to complete it.

The "One Thing" Is Worthy of Your Best

The "one thing" is the goal or dream God has called us to pursue. The good things are the opportunities that come our way but distract us from our mission. Is the "good thing" the enemy of the "one thing"? Don't settle for anything less than God's best. When God has given you a mission, go after it like a dog on a pork chop!

Business consultant Steve Seibold tells us in *Secrets of the World Class* that world-class performers use their ability to stay singularly focused on attaining a goal: "While average people haphazardly pursue loosely defined goals, champions concentrate on the attainment of a singular purpose with an intensity that borders on obsession."[56] The apostle Paul said it best: "This one thing I do, forgetting what lies behind, I press toward the upward call of God in Jesus Christ" (Philippians 3:13).

I believe the best way to stay focused is to have the expectation that, by the grace of God, we will achieve what he has called us to do. The confident expectation that "I can do all things through Christ who strengthens me" will see us through to the end.

Persevere by Referring to Your "Why"

I will talk more on perseverance in the next chapter. Persevering is the "stick to it till you do it" mentality that motivates us to stick with a goal until it is completed. A key motivator for persevering is to remember our "why."

Think of all the benefits and reasons you have decided to act. Put them in a first-person statement and repeat it often:

- ◇ "I am glorifying God."
- ◇ "I am fulfilling my purpose."
- ◇ "I am living my dreams."
- ◇ "I am growing as a person."
- ◇ "I am making the world a better place."

---

56 Steve Siebold, *Secrets of the World Class: Turning Mediocrity into Greatness* (Naperville, Ill.: Simple Truths, 2009), 6.

- ◇ "I am allowing God to accomplish his will in my life."
- ◇ "I am making my family stronger."
- ◇ "I am strengthening my future."
- ◇ "I am pursuing a good testimony to my faith."
- ◇ "I am helping others."
- ◇ "I am blessing others with my gifts and talents."
- ◇ "I am completing the mission."

Reminding ourselves of the reasons why we are doing something will give us motivation to complete the work.

IN THE "BEGINNING"

> "He also that is slothful in his work is brother to him who is a great waster."
>
> **PROVERBS 18:9 KJV**

All things great and small have a beginning; so take action! How many God-given goals and dreams have been wasted on inaction? God only knows. Don't waste what God wants you to work toward. What are some advantages of acting now?

Progress Begins

Five frogs are sitting on a log. Four decide to jump off. How many frogs are left on the log? The answer is five because deciding to jump off and jumping are two different things.

There is a difference between deciding and doing. The first frog off the log swims ahead of the others. When we act, the journey sometimes requires two steps forward and one step back, but we don't have to go back to square one. Even if we do have to start over, we have figured out a way not to do it. Action is progress. As has been said, "It takes action to get traction."

Fear Begins to Subside

The first time I got behind the steering wheel of a car, I was fearful. All kinds of thoughts went through my head: *What if I run into someone? What if the car breaks down? What if I run out of gas?* None of those things happened. The second time I drove a car, I was less afraid. Now I cannot imagine life without a vehicle. Action reduces fear.

Sometimes fear is good. Fear of getting burned keeps our hand out of the toaster. Fear of going to jail keeps us from breaking the law. Godly fear, which expresses itself in reverence and respect for the Almighty, is the foundation for Christian success. As Proverbs 9:10 explains, "The fear of the Lord is the beginning of wisdom, and knowledge of the holy is understanding."

Good fear protects us.

But fear of acting on our God-given dreams is neither holy nor healthy. It keeps us from moving forward and experiencing the abundant life that Jesus promised (John 10:10). The devil can deceive us into following our fears instead of acting in faith. Remember the acronym of FEAR:

False
Experiences
Appearing
Real

The good news is that when we act in faith, fear begins to subside. Each step forward puts fear farther behind us.

Momentum Begins to Grow

As a pastor, I liked seeing people at church. Sunday was a time to connect and catch up, but interacting with people for a few seconds on Sunday was not enough. People needed to be contacted during the week as well. This was usually done by phone calls. For me, the hardest part of making phone calls was dialing the first one. After the first, I had momentum to make another.

Someone once said it only takes a few small blocks under the wheels of a train to keep it from going. But when the blocks are removed and a train gets momentum, it can run over anything on the tracks and takes up to a mile to stop. Action builds momentum that can become an unstoppable force.

CONCLUSION

A man goes to church and prays, "God, I need a break. I need money to pay bills. I'm counting on you, God."

Having not received the money, the man returns to church a week later and prays, "God, about the money: I've been kind to my wife. I tuck my children into bed. I quit drinking, and I've been very good. Give me a break. Send me some money."

Another week goes by and no answer from God. The man returns to church and prays again.

"God, I don't seem to be getting through to you. The Bible says you own the cattle on a thousand hills. Can you give me a break and butcher a few and send me the cash?"

Suddenly the heavens open up, and thunderbolts and flashes of lightning are all around. A voice from heaven declares, "My son, give me a break. Get a job and go to work."

CAN DO; GO DO

- ◇ Do you see yourself as a person of action?
- ◇ What do you need to act on right now? Go!

CHAPTER 14

SMARTER:
USE THE SMARTER GOAL-SETTING
METHOD FOR TAKING ACTION

"A desire fulfilled is sweet to the soul."

PROVERBS 13:19A

"For a goal to matter, it has to stretch us."

MICHAEL HYATT

I began seminary with a goal of earning a master of divinity with biblical languages degree within three years. On January 1, 1990, my wife and I—having been married all of nine months—left Laurel, Maryland, and headed to Fort Worth, Texas. We drove a moving van with car in tow over twelve hundred miles in three days to move into an apartment, sight unseen.

Completing an MDiv in three years was very demanding. I took classes in the spring, fall, summer, and between semesters in order to stay on track for graduation. To pay bills, Carol worked full-time, I worked part-time, and friends from our home church and relatives helped us financially to make ends meet. In addition to work and school, we were also very involved in our local church.

During my last year of school, our son, Mason, was born.

Every night for the first year of his life, he would wake up between midnight and four in the morning. I would get up and give him a bottle of formula so Carol could sleep through the night before getting up to go to her job. We were like zombies, but we got through it.

In mid-December 1992, I graduated from Southwestern Baptist Theological Seminary with my degree. We achieved our goal! It was not easy, but I knew we could do it with God's help. We were determined, disciplined, and devoted to persevering and seeing it to the end.

Back then I knew very little about formal goal setting. I simply knew what I believed God wanted me to do and took action. I had a plan to accomplish it and a target date for completion. I also had supportive people to encourage and help.

A "SMARTER" WAY

In 1981, George Duran published an article in the trade periodical *Management Review* titled "There's a S.M.A.R.T. Way to Write Management's Goals and Objectives." In the paper, Mr. Duran explained the acronym SMART as it applied to goal setting in the workplace. His five original elements for goal setting were that the goal must be specific, measurable, assignable, realistic, and time-related.[57]

Over the years, the acronym has gone through a few iterations with some of the words being replaced and additional letters being added. I have found the SMARTER method of goal setting to be helpful in setting goals and succeeding in reaching them. I got the idea from Michael Hyatt in his book *Your Best*

---

57 G. T. Doran (1981). "There's A SMART Way to Write Management Goals and Objectives." *Management Review*, Vol. 70, Issue 11, pgs. 35-36

Year Ever: A Five-Step Plan for Achieving Your Best Year Ever.[58] I use the same acronym but a few different words and principles to describe the goal-setting method.

I apply the following qualifications in developing SMARTER goals:

Specific
Measurable
Attainable
Relevant
Time sensitive
Evaluated
Reviewable

Let's consider each one.

Specific

The "S" in SMARTER stands for "specific." That is, the goal must be clearly defined. Studies show that the more specific we are in goal setting, the more likely we are to reach it. When setting a goal, we must think about who, what, when, where, why, and how we plan to reach it.

For example, suppose we have a goal of reading the Bible. Great, but it is not specific. When, where, why, and how will we read the Bible? The SMARTER goal may read like this: "Beginning on [set date], I will read the Bible for fifteen minutes per day when I get up in the morning and complete it in twelve months. This will help me become a better follower of Christ."

Notice how the goal of reading through the Bible has a specific beginning, time of day, amount of time each day, end date, and a reason why someone would want to read it.

---

58 Michael S. Hyatt, *Your Best Year Ever: A Five-Step Plan For Achieving Your Best Year Ever* (Grand Rapids, MI: Baker Books, 2018).

Measurable

The second letter of the acronym stands for "measurable." How will we know if we have reached our goal if there is no way of measuring our progress? Saying, "I will read the Bible for fifteen minutes per day and finish in a year" is measurable or quantitative. We are either reading or not reading the Bible for fifteen minutes per day. In order to make a goal measurable, ask questions such as "How much?" or "How many?"

Developing measurable goals is like making a cake. A baker has to measure certain ingredients, mix them in a bowl, and pour the batter in a pan. Then, the cake has to bake at the right temperature for a certain amount of time. If the measurements of ingredients, time, and temperature are off, the cake will not turn out right. Measurable ingredients make for great dessert! Forgive the cheesy food analogy.

Attainable

Goals should stretch us without breaking our will to achieve them.

In 1508, Pope Julius II commissioned Michelangelo to paint the ceiling of the Sistine Chapel in the Vatican. Michelangelo considered himself a sculptor, not a painter, and did not want to take on the task, but the pope insisted. The artist labored for four years. He climbed scaffolding to the ceiling of the church, over sixty feet high, and painted on his back. His sight was permanently damaged from the paint dripping into his eyes. He eventually finished the approximately 132-by-44-foot ceiling! Today, over five hundred years later, the chapel attracts over five million visitors yearly. Michelangelo is reported to have said, "The greater danger for most of us is not that our aim is too high and we miss it, but that it is too low and we hit it."[59]

---

59   https://leadershipnow.com/visionquotes2.html

Placing the bar too low takes away the challenge and the thrill of achievement. Yet if we set the bar too high, we will become frustrated, and morale will decrease. We need to find our sweet spot.

Going back to our example of reading through the Bible: Saying, "I want to read the entire Bible by tomorrow" is specific and measurable but not attainable because it takes longer than twenty-four hours to read in its entirety. A year is attainable and will be a stretch for most of us. FYI: according to Crossway, it takes seventy-four hours and twenty-eight minutes to read through the good book.[60]

In *Your Best Year Ever*, Michael Hyatt describes three zones when it comes to goal setting: the comfort zone, the discomfort zone, and the delusional zone. Comfort-zone goals are easily attainable but do not challenge us to reach higher. Hyatt says, "For a goal to matter, it has to stretch us."[61]

The other extreme is "delusional" goals. These are goals that are impossible to achieve. Hyatt believes these do not inspire us to do our best but, to the contrary, ensure failure.[62] Goals in the discomfort zone will stretch us without breaking us. Discomfort-zone goals can trigger fear, uncertainty, and doubt and yet inspire us to continue reaching until they are attained.

Relevant

Will our goal help us reach our God-given dreams? Will it help us fulfill our life purpose? If the answer is no, then it is probably not a relevant goal. Relevant goals should align with our Christian walk and witness. In fact, it is not too strong to say that if our goal is outside of the will of God, he will not help us

---

60 https://www.crossway.org/articles/infographic-you-can-read-more-of-the-bible-than-you-think.
61 *Your Best Year Ever*, 137.
62 Ibid, 140.

achieve it because it does not align with his perfect plan for us.

Relevant goals should also complement our season of life. For example, a goal of traveling in an RV and visiting all fifty states while working, parenting, and paying off student loans will probably lead to more frustration than fulfillment because the timing is not right. It is at best a wish, not a goal.

When determining if a goal is relevant, ask yourself, *Does this goal align with my beliefs and values? Does this goal help me reach my God-given potential in Christ?*

Time Sensitive

Having a deadline creates a challenge and adds focus to completing a task. Using our example of reading the Bible in its entirety, a one-year deadline will help us develop the habit of daily Bible reading. If we don't put a deadline to completion, it could take five or ten years—or never get finished! A deadline marks the fulfillment of the timeline for completing important goals and tasks.

Evaluated

As the old adage goes, "You can't expect what you don't inspect." Using a SMARTER method for goal setting allows for evaluating progress daily, weekly, or monthly until the goal is accomplished. Why? Because it is easy to put off till tomorrow what we should do today!

Reviewable

We have to plan our work and work our plan. If our plan is not working, we need to adjust it. Goals should be set with every intention of completing them, but life happens.

When reviewing your plan, ask yourself, *Am I still motivated to accomplish this goal? Why am I not on track to complete it? Am I devoting enough time to it? What do I need to change in order to accomplish it? Who can help me get back on track? Why did I set this goal in the first place?* Asking questions will help clarify the "why" and help us think of some new "hows" to complete the task.

The SMARTER goal method is a guide, or a mental map, to help establish and prioritize important goals. The following practices provide additional information and a process to help clarify goals and attain them.

REACHING "SMARTER" GOALS

"A goal without a plan is just a wish," said French writer Antoine de Saint-Exupery.[63]

My brother is a master electrician. He can wire anything. When the lights go off at my house, I get him on Skype real fast. He has a van full of tools and all kinds of wire gadgets and gizmos when he goes to a jobsite. He doesn't need every tool for every job, but he needs the right tool for the particular job. The following "tools" are part of the equipment for reaching our God-given goals. Use the ones that particularly work for you.

Picturing Our Life Wheel

Let's take a look at the eight areas that influence our lives: spiritual, physical, emotional, intellectual, relational, vocational, financial, and lifestyle. Is there an area that is out of balance? In what areas is it time to make the most improvement? What progress would we like to make in these areas in the next week, month, quarter, six months, year, and five years? What do we need to do today to start the process?

---

63 https://quotefancy.com/quote/7281/Antoine-de-Saint-Exup-ry-A-goal-without-a-plan-is-just-a-wish

Praying

Praying here involves asking God for wisdom in setting and prioritizing goals. As James writes, "If anyone lacks wisdom, let him ask of God, who gives to all generously and without reproach, and it shall be given him" (James 1:5).

In addition to praying for help in setting goals, we can pray for help in completing goals. A godly goal will draw us closer to God and cause us to depend on him. Goal setting and achieving can be a spiritual act of discipleship when our hearts are right and our motives are to please God. In addition, we should always remember to pray and thank God when our goal is completed.

If we "pray without ceasing" throughout the entire process of making and reaching our goals, reaching our goals then becomes a God-honoring way of becoming more like Christ (1 Thessalonians 5:17).

Pondering Options and Picking

There is something in every area of life that can be improved. Think through each category of the life wheel and pick something in the area that you believe God wants you to improve right now. Would you like to grow in your spiritual life by developing your prayer life? Set a SMARTER goal to pray daily at a specific time and for a certain amount of time—and start. Find prayer tools and Bible verses to help.

Perhaps in the area of relationships you would like to spend more time with your spouse. Set a goal to have a date night once a week and go away together once a quarter. Make it a point to increase your daily time together.

How are you doing in the area of finances? Do you need to save more money for retirement? Make an appointment with a financial planner and start funding a retirement account. Do you have a budget? Are you living within or below your income? Listen to Dave Ramsey or other voices that give solid money-management advice.

As you look over your life wheel, you may notice that some areas need significant improvement. Don't judge yourself; adjust yourself. Set two or three SMARTER goals in the area of greatest need, and make it your priority to do better. If you are an "overachiever," set more.

Planning

As mentioned in the previous chapter, it is necessary to plan out a strategy for goal achievement. What will it take to get us to the goal? How long do we believe it will take? How much will it cost? Who will we need to help us?

Plans relieve the pressure of the unknown. Keep in mind that plans can change and often do, but make a plan.

Prioritizing

Many goal-setting proponents make a distinction between immediate, short-range, and long-range goals. Immediate goals are things we would like to get done in one day to two weeks. They are at the top of our daily "to-do" sheet. It could be anything from cleaning the house to making a phone call or finishing a book we started reading last year.

Short-term goals usually take from one to six months or up to a year to complete. For instance, losing twenty pounds or paying off a maxed-out credit card cannot be done immediately. Some goals need daily attention and take longer to achieve than others.

Long-term goals are tied to questions we ask about the future, such as "Where would I like to be in five to ten years? What would I like to be doing? What are some things God is leading me to achieve and experience before he calls me home?"

Long-term goals are reached by setting immediate goals and short-term goals that support achieving the long-term goal. Long-term goals are not completed immediately, but we have to make immediate plans to achieve them.

For example, several years ago I went on a preaching tour in India with a mission team. Being immersed in a completely different culture was a tremendous experience. I spoke to hundreds of people in large cities and little towns about the gospel of Christ and saw many come to faith. I think back on the time fondly.

The trip, however, was the culmination of a process that started a year before. There were funds to raise, visas to obtain, shots to take, itineraries to schedule, travel plans to coordinate, and all of this while pastoring my church. I had to make immediate and short-term goals in order to achieve the long-term quest of ministering on the other side of the globe. God honored the goal, and he also blessed the plan.

Putting It In Writing

Author Darren Hardy said, "Don't think it; ink it!" We make notes of things that are important to us and want to remember. Goals are very important! Neuropsychologists observe that the brain is constantly evaluating what to remember and what to discard. Individuals who write thoughts down have a better memory for material they produce themselves than material they have merely read. This is known as a "generation effect" on the brain.[64]

Writing down goals gives them more validity than merely thinking about wanting to do something someday. The act of writing it down and seeing it on the page can anchor the brain to achieve the task.

---

64 https://www.forbes.com/sites/markmurphy/2018/04/15/neuroscience-explains-why-you-need-to-write-down-your-goals-if-you-actually-want-to-achieve-them/#33d68e727905.

Powerful Desire

A detailed plan with written goals coupled with a whatever-it-takes mindset is essential to reaching our goals. Business expert Brian Buffini stated, "If you want to live your best life, be relentless in your pursuit of it! Face your fears, change your mind-set, and adopt the habits that will lead you to success."[65] Sometimes, success comes down to how much we want it. How do we know if we have a burning desire? When the goals we have actually have *us*.

Place of Prominence

Write out your goals (or type them) and place them where you constantly see them. Put them beside your bed at night so they are the last thing you see before falling asleep and the first thing you see when you wake up. If you want to lose weight, write your desired number and tape it on the refrigerator door and the bathroom mirror. If you want to be more loving toward your spouse, place "I love you" post-it notes around the house. Writing down goals is rooted in science and practical experience.

Process and review your goals daily: review, review, review. If you are like me, your memory bucket leaks. Great goals can go by the wayside if we do not constantly remind ourselves of their importance. I have attended goal-setting workshops, written down great goals, placed them in a binder, and neglected to follow up. I remember finding one of the notebooks months later and rereading the goals. In the back of my mind I was thinking, *I meant to do that! How did I forget?*

Constantly reviewing our goals has at least two benefits. First, the goal becomes ingrained in our subconscious to the point of becoming a preoccupation. What we constantly think about we are inclined to act on. A second reason for regularly reviewing

---

65 Brian Buffini, *The Emigrant Edge*, (Howard Books, New York, 2017) pg. 201.

goals is to check progress to see if we are still on schedule to complete the specific goal in a measured amount of time.

People

"It takes a team to complete the dream," as the adage goes. God has made us to live in community. That is, we are conditioned to need and want the help of other people. Scripture is full of examples to support this truth. Moses was supported by Aaron. King David was friends with Jonathan. Elijah was served by Elisha. Jesus had his disciples. We will benefit from the help of others in reaching our God-given goals.

When I lost forty-five pounds, I asked my cousin to be my accountability partner. He was one of my most fit cousins, so I figured he was doing something right. Each week, I would tell him how much weight I lost or didn't lose. I took "selfies" of me on a treadmill in order to show him, and remind me, that I was serious about the goal. He would send texts saying, "Go for a walk" or "How much weight have you lost?" or "You can do it!" His exhortation and encouragement helped a lot.

In the process of writing this book, I have asked friends and relatives to pray for its completion. People I work with will ask, "How is the book coming along?" I appreciate their desire to see me succeed. The saying is true: "If you see a turtle on a fence post, you know he didn't get there by himself." We need other people to encourage us, challenge us, believe in us, and pray for us as we pursue our goals.

Proper Practice

It has been said that "practice makes perfect." That is not exactly so. If someone is practicing incorrectly, they are merely forming a bad habit. The key is to learn the proper way to achieve the goal and then master the required skills through proper practice. This is true of sports, music, relationships, and career development. There are best practices that propel us to the top. Learn them and master them.

The pursuit of goals should include the desire to master the steps in the process of reaching what we set out to do. Great performers are great practicers. It's been said, "Don't practice until you get it right. Practice until you can't get it wrong." There are no shortcuts to mastery. It is the daily habit of proper practice that brings phenomenal results.

Persistent, Consistent, and Relentless Action

Goal attainment needs daily persistence, consistent action, and relentless pursuit. A small hammer can break a huge rock if we hit it hard enough and long enough. A small axe can fell a large tree if we keep chopping. Today is a good day to do something toward reaching our goals.

In the *New York Times* best-selling book *Great by Choice*, authors Jim Collins and Morten T. Hansen refer to "fanatical discipline" as one of the core practices of successful enterprises. Companies, organizations, teams, and individuals that achieve great results over a long period are able to consistently deliver high performance in difficult times and hold back in good times.[66]

To illustrate the point, they contrast the expeditions of two explorers and their teams' journeys to the South Pole. Robert F. Scott and Roald Amundsen and their teams set out in October 1911 to be the first in modern history to reach the pole. Amundsen and his team reached the destination on December 15, thirty-four days ahead of Scott. Sadly, Scott and what was left of his team perished on the return trip, never making it home.

There were key reasons why one team made it home and one did not. One reason was that Amundsen had a persistent, consistent, and relentless goal of daily progress. He would never

---

66 Jim Collins and Morten T. Hansen, *Great by Choice* (New York: Harper Collins, 2011), 65.

drive his men too hard in good weather and carefully kept them from plowing through to exhaustion in bad weather. Amundsen set a goal to travel fifteen to twenty miles per day, good weather or bad. They averaged 15.5 miles per day.

By contrast, Scott would drive his team to exhaustion on good days and stay in his tent for days on end when he believed the weather conditions were not suitable to hike. Scott's lack of consistent persistence caused him to lag behind Amundsen's team and contributed to the demise of Scott's own team.

In order to reach our goals, it is important to develop the habit of persistent, consistent, and relentless action.

Persevering

An old saying goes, "It takes ten years to become an overnight success!" The length of the journey to reaching our goals can seem like ten years, and ten years is a long time. That is why perseverance is so important.

The ninety-ninety rule of computer coding was popularized by Tom Cargill of Bell Labs. He stated: "The first 90 percent of the code accounts for the first 90 percent of the development time. The remaining 10 percent of the code accounts for the other 90 percent of the development time."[67] Don't quit! Push for the last 10 percent that will give you a 90 percent return on investing in your God-given goals.

The world is full of people who quit just before they reached their goals. Don't be like them! Be like the apostle Paul when he said, "I press on toward the goal for the prize of the upward call of God in Christ Jesus" (Philippians 3:14 ESV). God-given goals are usually reached through trial, errors, setbacks, and comebacks. Perseverance teaches us to hold on to God and hang in the fight.

Beverly Buffini was watching the 1976 Olympics on her

---

67   https://thenewstack.io/code-n00b-ol-ninety-ninety

television set in Montgomery, Alabama.[68] She was in awe of Bruce Jenner, an American athlete who no one knew much about and who won the men's decathlon for Team USA. A dream began to develop in Beverly: she wanted to go to the Olympics.

Beverly was a gifted athlete in volleyball but not naturally self-confident. She did not realize the value she brought to her team and did not believe she could contribute to the sport of women's volleyball. In her junior year of high school, Bev's parents took her to a volleyball camp. At the end of camp, a coach from California told her she had a lot of potential and could go far in the sport. Those words resonated with Beverly. She began to work harder to be a great volleyball player.

As she was approaching graduation, Beverly had not received any offers from colleges to play volleyball. Though not recruited, she did not quit. She sent letters to schools and received an offer for a full-ride scholarship from the University of Alabama. She played on the women's volleyball team for two years, until the school decided to cut the program.

Beverly believed she could contribute to a volleyball program, so she wrote more letters to universities. Again, she received a response from one school, the University of Tennessee. Beverly did not disappoint. The first year, her team won the SEC championship and she was named MVP. Before she graduated, she was named first team All American, one of twelve women in the country. She was eventually inducted into the University of Tennessee's sports hall of fame and had her jersey retired.

Her accomplishments in women's volleyball were monumental, but Beverly still had a dream to go to the Olympics. She remembered the words that coach had told her as a high school junior: she had the potential to go far. She decided to become a coach at West Point for a year so she could train for the

---

[68] Brian Buffini Show podcast 187, *"I Can, I Will, I Believe"* with Beverly Buffini

Olympic team. As Olympic tryouts neared, she had not received an invitation. She went back to a tried-and-true method: she wrote letters and had friends write letters to the USA Olympic team. She was eventually offered the opportunity to try out for the team—if she would stop writing letters!

Out of sixty-four women, nine were selected, and Beverly was one of them. She was a member of the USA Women's National Volleyball Team from 1985 to 1988. She and the team won a bronze medal at the 1987 Pan American Games, and Beverly was an alternate on the 1988 Olympic team. Having a dream, believing she could, and persevering until she did were the recipe for success. Persistent, consistent, relentless!

Production

It has been said, "The fifty-second law of leadership is 'production,' and the other fifty-one don't matter." In reaching our goals, we must constantly ask ourselves if we are producing results. If not, why not? Procrastination? A loss of focus, laziness, or loss of desire? Have we plateaued and need help? Is God leading in a new direction?

When our activity is not producing the desired result, we need to seriously assess the situation. Lack of production makes us feel like we are not making progress. This can lead to frustration and loss of focus. Asking ourselves, "What result is my activity producing?" helps us measure our progress and make adjustments as necessary.

Power from God

Jesus said, "Apart from me you can do nothing" (John 15:5). We cannot succeed apart from God's help; nor would we want to. It is important to remember that reaching our God-given potential through Christ *is* the goal. The personal goals God has for us are a means to make us more like Jesus: "For whom he foreknew, them he also predestined to be conformed to the likeness of Christ" (Romans 8:29).

Pursuing our God-given goals should deepen our prayer life, develop our character, inspire encouragement from devoted friends, and increase our dependence on God. If success does not draw us closer to God, we are not truly succeeding.

Positive Attitude

Another verse worth repeating: "Count it all joy, my brethren, when you encounter various trials, knowing that the testing of your faith produces patience" (James 1:2).

Pursuing goals should make us glad, not grumpy!

I was at the hardware store recently, looking for materials to complete a home project. It was my third trip, and I was a little perturbed. I grabbed a cart on the way in and was intent on getting what I needed and getting back to the house.

I was speeding down an aisle when I noticed that a little boy was in my way and would not move. I thought, *Surely he will get out of my way*, but the closer I got, the more entrenched he became. In fact, he stood in the middle of the aisle, feet anchored to the floor, like an adolescent superhero daring me to try to get past him. There was enough room to go around him, so I skirted out of his way and proceeded to where I needed to go.

As I went around, I heard the boy's mother say, "Why didn't you get out of the man's way?"

To which the boy replied, "He looked mean."

Bravo to the boy who stood up to the bully with a shopping cart! Shame on me for having a bad attitude.

Keeping a positive attitude is essential to growing into our goals. Goals should make us grateful, not hateful. Goals should free us to the possibility of greater faith, not frustrate us in the work. Someone once said, "Of all the seven dwarfs, only one was Happy." Be happy in life. A good attitude is infinitely better than a bad one.

Patting Ourselves on the Back

We reached our goal. We completed the task. We crossed the finish line. That is great! Now what?

Reward yourself! Psychological research has shown that God has wired our brains to respond to rewards. We give prizes, trophies, and awards because people want to be recognized for their achievements. In fact, if we do not reward ourselves, the lack of acknowledgment can become de-motivating.

When you reach a weight goal, buy a new outfit. When you complete a project at work, have a luncheon. How you reward yourself is up to you, but don't sabotage yourself from future success by failing to recognize, in a tangible way, what you were able to accomplish by God's grace and your hard work.

CONCLUSION

Setting SMARTER goals is a great method of thinking and planning through our God-given goals and dreams. Putting into practice the "how to" of reaching and achieving our potential is very doable if we have a "do-able" attitude. Remember, growing to be like Christ *is* the goal.

CAN DO; GO DO

Review the SMARTER goal method. What God-sized goal will you begin to act on?

SECTION 5

"ALL THINGS"

God will help us do all the things he has called us to do if we seek to understand his will for our lives and how he has shaped us.

"I can do **all things** through Christ who strengthens me."

CHAPTER 15
URIM AND THUMMIM: HOW TO DISCOVER GOD'S WILL FOR YOUR LIFE

"For it is God who works in you, both to will and to work for His good pleasure."

PHILIPPIANS 2:13

"To know the will of God is the greatest knowledge. To do the will of God is the greatest achievement."

GEORGE W. TRUETT

There is no true success outside of the will of God, and no failure within it.

Question: What are the "all things" God says we can do? Answer: everything in God's will and plan for us to do! Ephesians 2:10 tells us, "For we are His workmanship created in Christ Jesus for good works, which God has prepared beforehand that we should walk in them." Paul promised the Philippians, "He that began a good work in you will be faithful to complete it till the day of Christ Jesus" (Philippians 1:6).

God's will is what he wants us to do. His plan is how we accomplish his will.

From the beginning of time, people have sought various

ways to discern the divine will. Ancient Assyrians looked at the entrails of animals. The Greeks and Romans practiced augury, a ritual for discerning the will of Zeus by observing the flights of birds. As misguided as we think these archaic approaches are, we should recognize their performers' desire for a power beyond themselves to give direction to life's choices.

Scripture also gives examples of methods people used to determine God's will. The Old Testament book of Judges tells the story of how Gideon used the dew on the ground and a fleecy garment (Judges 6:33–40). Aaron, Israel's first high priest, used the "Urim and the Thummim" when there was no clear direction from the Torah (Exodus 28:30). These objects were gemstones the high priest carried on the breastplate of his ephod. The Bible is scant on exactly how the high priest deciphered God's will from the Urim and Thummim. Some scholars surmise they may have been thrown like dice. Others propose they had a crystal composition that lit up to reveal God's will.

The New Testament also recounts instances of seeking the will of God. The early apostles "cast lots" when seeking a replacement for Judas. On rare occasions, God spoke through dreams and visions. For example, Peter was shown in a vision from God that he was to proclaim the gospel to Cornelius the Gentile (Acts 10). These scriptural examples were effective then, but how do we determine God's will for our life now?

As a pastor, I was often asked by church members, "What does God want me/us to do?" The questions ran the gamut of everything from what type of floor to install in the new family life center to God's choice for a spouse, or what career one ought to pursue. The good news is that people want to know what God thinks about every circumstance of life. The bad news is that asking a preacher is no guarantee of a right answer!

On one occasion, I was asked by a church member if it was God's will for her to sell a piece of property. We were good friends and would sometimes kid each other. I told her she had done pretty well for herself without my advice, and it was probably not a good idea to take financial guidance from a poor pastor. She laughed but persisted in asking. So I told her to sell the property and give the money to the church. She didn't.

We want to make our lives count. We want to reach our God-given potential through Christ. Great! But what is it God wants us to do? What is God's will for our lives? This chapter will give guidance on getting clarity in discovering these answers.

CATEGORIES OF THE WILL OF GOD

To begin our discussion, it is important to understand the different categories or aspects of God's will. Let's mention three.

God's sovereign will: God can do whatever he wills. He is Lord of the universe. Humans cannot change it, nor can we stop it. We have to accept it. For instance, in his own time and in his own way, Jesus will return according to God's perfect timing. Our job is to be ready and serve him whether he returns in our lifetime or not.

God's preceptive or moral will: In Scripture, God has given us his laws, precepts, statutes, and commands. They are God's rules for us to live by, even though we may break them. To a large extent, God's will for our lives is already revealed to us in the Bible. We simply need to do what he says. When we obey God by following the rules laid out for us in Scripture, we are following his preceptive will.

God's particular will: Throughout the Bible, we see instances of how God reveals his will to people. Sometimes it is dramatic, as in the call of Abraham (Genesis 12). Other times, it can be as mundane as someone going about their daily tasks, as in the case of the woman who went to a well to get water and met Jesus (John 4). Whatever the case may be, there are some considerations in relation to God's will and our lives, which I will expand on in the following section.

CONSIDERATIONS IN RELATION TO GOD'S WILL AND OUR LIVES

God Has a Plan for Our Lives

God's plan for us is a better plan than what we have for ourselves. As Jeremiah 29:11 says, "I know the plans I have for you, declares the Lord. Plans to prosper you and not to harm you. Plans to give you a hope and a future."

God did not create us to leave us alone and hope we turn out the best we can. No! He loves us and is concerned with the details of our lives. Jesus said, "Are not five sparrows sold for two coins, and not one of them is forgotten by God. But even the very hairs of your head are numbered. Fear not; you are worth more than many sparrows" (Luke 12:6–7).

Pastor George Sweeting wisely stated, "It makes a great deal of sense that the God who is the master Designer, the Creator and Sustainer of the universe, should also be interested in the plan of our lives. He who hung the worlds in space must be concerned about us, His creation."[69]

God's Plan for Our Lives May Take Several Pathways

God's will for us may take us through several vocations as well as locations. His plan may involve many plans. Statistics show that, on average, Americans move about eleven times and

---

69 George Sweeting, *How to Discover the Will of God* (Chicago: Moody Bible Institute, 1975), 17.

work at eleven different jobs. Additionally, we have interests, hobbies, the desire for a spouse, and the need to be a part of a local church. Some aspects of the will of God may be meant for a season of life while walking with God for a lifetime.

We can look at the life of David, a man after God's own heart (1 Samuel 13:14), and see how the will of God for an individual life can take several paths. He was born in Bethlehem, lived in various locations in Judea, and established his kingly residence in Jerusalem. He was a shepherd, warrior, son, husband, father, musician, poet, and king of Israel. Similar to David's, our life books may have many chapters. Several vocations and different locations, yet God was guiding in each.

God Wants Us to Know His Will

The Lord promises in Psalms 32:8, "I will instruct you and teach you the way you should go. My eye will guide you."

Many believers are not experiencing God's will to the fullest. It could be our own doing: lack of faith, lack of knowledge, or lack of obedience. Or it could be that God is not ready to disclose his plan. The key is to keep believing and to walk in the light he has shown us until we receive his peace. To use a saying from Dr. Martin Luther King, God doesn't want us to walk misguided in a world full of guided missiles. He loves us too much not to want us to know his will!

God does not promise to show us every detail of his will for us on the front end. If he did, we would not need to walk by faith. He does promise to light our way as we walk with him.

Have faith that God will shed the light of his will in your heart.

God's Will Is Always Best for Us

Sometimes we are not clear on the will of God because we are not doing what he has already told us to do. We are sometimes guilty of not pursuing his will for our lives because our rebellious natures can trick us into thinking our way is better. In short, we want to have our own way instead of God having his way in us.

Don't settle for what you want; strive for God's best. As Romans 12:2 exhorts, "Be not conformed to this world, but be transformed by the renewing of your mind, that you may prove what is that good, and acceptable and perfect will of God."

Don't be deceived into settling for anything less.

God's Will Is Revealed in a Relationship with Him

The closer we sit to the fire, the warmer we get. The closer we get to the light, the clearer we see. Psalms 36:9 explains, "For with you is the fountain of life; in your light do we see light."

God's revealed will for our lives is a fringe benefit of loving him. Our greatest need is not to know God's will for our lives but to willingly love God with the lives we have.

In his best-selling book *Experiencing God*, author Henry Blackaby presents a tremendous truth:

> God is far more interested in a love relationship with you than He is in what you do for Him. His desire is for you to love Him. As He walks alongside you, He will guide you into specific activities. But even as you do those things, He will be the One working through you to accomplish His purposes. He is all you need. Christ in you is your way; He is your map. When you follow His leadership one day at a time, you will always be right in the middle of God's will.[70]

Similarly, theologian Leslie D. Weatherhead said, "I am quite sure that the greatest help available in discerning the will of God

---

70 Henry Blackaby and Claude King, *Experiencing God: Knowing and Doing the Will of God* (Nashville: B&H Publishing Group, 2008), 39.

is reached when we deepen our friendship with him. Those who know God are the quickest and surest at discerning his will."[71]

Knowing and Doing God's Will Brings a Life of Favor and Blessing

Psalms 37:4 declares: "Delight yourself in the Lord, and he will give you the desires of your heart." Walking in the will of God brings joy, fulfillment, purpose, and soul satisfaction. When God's "will to" becomes our "want to," we are blessed.

CONDITIONS FOR DISCERNING THE WILL OF GOD

A condition is an arrangement that must exist before results can take place. A condition is also a proper state or disposition of mind and heart for understanding to take place.

I think the second definition is closer to the mark when it comes to discerning the will of God. We will never meet all of the conditions perfectly. Neither are they boxes to check off of a "to do" list. They are more of a disposition that facilitates awareness. The following conditions will allow us to discern the will of God more clearly and quickly.

Saved

The first step to knowing the will of God is to be related to him in a saving way. Chapter 11 tells us how we can be rightly related to God through Jesus Christ. The head coach of a basketball team trains the players on *his* team, *not* the players on the other team. If you want God to train you and develop you, then join his team! As 2 Peter 3:9 explains, "For God is willing

---

[71] Leslie D. Weatherhead, *The Will of God* (Nashville: Festival Books/Abington, 3rd Printing, 1977), 47.

that none should perish, but that all might come to repentance."

Jesus has done everything necessary for us to join God's team and receive his direction. Believe the Bible when it says, "For God has not appointed us to wrath, but to obtain salvation through our Lord Jesus Christ" (1 Thessalonians 5:9).

Seeking

God says, "You will seek me and find me when you search for me with your whole heart" (Jeremiah 29:13).

Both Old and New Testaments reiterate the willing necessity of believers to "seek the Lord and his strength; seek his presence continually" (Psalms 105:4 ESV). Scripture does contain rare examples of God revealing himself to people when they were not (at least to our knowledge) seeking him: Abraham, Jacob, and Moses come to mind. God is sovereign! He is free to act as he wills. The overwhelming thrust of Scripture is to seek God.

God tells us to seek him because his ways are different from ours (Isaiah 55:6–9). There is usually a discovery process through which God reveals his will. In times of prayer and reflection, conversations with godly friends, and time in the Scripture, God reveals the direction we believe he is leading. He gives impressions through the Holy Spirit that we should act upon. With his direction comes faith to decide and a determination to act. As Psalms 34:10 explains, "The lions may grow weak and weary, but those who seek the Lord lack no good thing."

Seeking the will of God should be done with a sincere (whole) heart. Sometimes we decide what we want to do, then ask God to bless it. In these instances, we aren't sincere in seeking his will. Rather, we are more concerned with getting his stamp of approval for what we have already decided to do. Sincerity means truly wanting what God has for us.

Surrendered

Jesus told his disciples, "If anyone would follow me, let him deny himself daily, and pick up his cross and follow me" (Matthew 16:24).

In the Garden of Gethsemane, the night before Jesus was crucified, he prayed three times to the Father that he would not have to drink the cup of the cross. The prayer of the Savior ended with "Not as I will, but as you will" (Matthew 26:39). When we have surrendered our will to the will of the Father, we are in a position to hear more clearly and to act more courageously.

George Müller was a famous preacher and pastor in the 1800s. During the years of his ministry, he preached in Europe as well as the United States. He started a printing house for Christian literature and developed Christian schools and orphanages in Bristol, England. He was known for his great dependence on God through prayer. His charitable trust, still in existence today, does not advertise for donations, yet they continue to receive generous contributions. They too choose to carry on Müller's legacy of praying and letting the Lord provide.

Müller's famous pamphlet *How to Ascertain the Will of God* is included at the end of this chapter. His first rule asserts, "I seek at the beginning to get my heart into such a state that it has no will of its own in regard to a given matter. . . . When one is truly in this state, it is usually but a little way to the knowledge of what his will is."[72] God led Müller to do many things in many places because he was surrendered to performing the will of God.

Separated

Paul told the Thessalonians, "For this is the will of God, your sanctification: that you should abstain from sexual immorality, that each one of you should know how to possess his own vessel

---

72 See principle 1 of *How to Ascertain the Will of God* at the end of the chapter.

in sanctification and honor" (1 Thessalonians 4:3).

I mentioned it before, and it's worth repeating: When we are saved by Christ, we are "sanctified" or "set apart" for God. As the Spirit of Christ transforms us on the inside, we become more Christ like in our attitudes and actions. God does all the work in saving us. We must cooperate with him as he "sanctifies" us.

Think of plaque in the body's arteries that causes blockages that lead to a heart attack. Little microscopic goblets of fat and cholesterol attach themselves to the walls of the arteries and decrease the flow of oxygen-rich blood. The blockages build up over time, caused by a host of contributing factors, like poor diet, lack of exercise, smoking, stress, or genetic disposition, to name a few. We may or may not recognize the symptoms, but the results are the same: heart trouble!

Not separating ourselves from the sins of the world causes spiritual "heart trouble." If we continue in it, over time, it will block us from discerning God's will. The good and acceptable and perfect will of God is understood when we offer our bodies to God and our minds are renewed by the Spirit of God (Romans 12:1–2).

Serving

Some believe they should wait until God tells them what to do before doing anything. Don't wait! God has already told us to serve him, and "to him who knows to do good and does not, to him it is sin" (James 4:16). Jesus came to serve. He expects us to do the same.

Ask your pastor where you can serve in the church. Volunteer to serve in a community organization. As Christian author Henrietta Mears said, "It is difficult to steer a parked car, so get moving."[73]

Many have discovered that when they start doing something, God begins to show them something. He may show them how

---

73 https://www.inspiringquotes.us/author/6552-henrietta-mears

to do it better or how to get others to help. He may impart some wisdom from the experience, or he may tell them to do something else. I learned a lot about human nature not from reading books on psychology but from the wisdom received from God through serving people.

Stewardship

Our lives are on loan from God, and we have a responsibility to make the most of them for his glory and the good of others. A steward is someone who has been entrusted with caring for something that belongs to another. He or she is expected to prize it, protect it, promote it, and produce good fruit from it. As Jesus declared, "Now listen, you who say, 'Today or tomorrow we will go to this or that city, spend a year there, carry on business and make money.' Why, you do not even know what will happen tomorrow. What is your life? You are a mist that appears for a little while and then vanishes. Instead, you ought to say, 'If it is the Lord's will, we will live and do this or that'" (James 4:13–15).

When we realize we belong to God and our lives are on loan from God, we will have greater impetus to walk in the will of God.

God wants us to know his will, but the timing belongs to him. A saved, seeking, surrendered, separated, serving, and stewardship-centered life are conditions of the mind and heart that help us discern the will of God. In addition, God has channels by which he shows us his will.

CORE COMPONENTS FOR HOW GOD'S WILL IS DISCLOSED

Core components are the "must-haves" in order to achieve desired outcomes. For instance, the core components of an airplane are the body, wings, tail, engine, and landing gear. Without them, a plane cannot fly. What are the core components of discerning the will of God?

The Holy Spirit

Jesus told his disciples, "When the Spirit of truth comes, he will guide you into all the truth" (John 16:13 ESV).

We are not alone in the process of discovering God's will. In fact, it is more accurate to say that we don't discover God's will, but rather God reveals his will to us. We can't find spiritual truth on our own. God has to take the initiative to show us, and he does!

Billy Graham is undoubtedly the most well-known American evangelist of his time. He preached to millions of people in hundreds of countries. He was a counselor to presidents and friend to everyone. Reverend Graham conducted over four hundred preaching crusades in a span of fifty-plus years. How did he decide where to preach? One of his key guidelines (see the end of the chapter for the full list) was the inner "prompting of the Holy Spirit."

God the Holy Spirit may speak to us in many ways: for example, in "the still small voice"; through an impression or a burden to do something; or a "godly desire." But how do we know it is God leading us and not our own selfish desires—or the devil trying to lead us astray? We must remember that we are to "test the spirits, to see if they be of God" (1 John 4:1). God gives us the following spiritual tools to help confirm the leading of the Spirit in understanding God's will.

Bible

Paul wrote to the apostle Timothy, "All Scripture is given by inspiration of God and is profitable for doctrine, reproof, correction, and training in righteousness, that the man of God may be complete; thoroughly equipped for every good work" (2

Timothy 3:16).

The Spirit of God uses the Word of God to teach us the ways of God and reveal to us the will of God. The Bible—God's Word—must be studied in context with the whole of Scripture to derive the proper meaning and act accordingly. As we study Scripture and become more and more familiar with what it says, we have every confidence that God will guide us in the day-to-day decisions of life as well as the life-changing decisions that shape our destinies.

The Bible is God's perfect revelation of precepts, principles, perspective, promises, prophecy, prohibitions, praises, and prayers of pure truth. When it comes to the will of God, our first question should not be "What does God want me to do?" The better question is "What does God tell me to do in his Word?" Why? Because much of God's will for you and me has already been revealed in the mandates of the Bible.

> "Teach me, O Lord, to follow your decrees; and I will keep them to the end."
>
> **PSALMS 119:33**

Missionary J. Oswald Sanders said, "We learn God's will, mainly, not by impulses and impressions, but by the prayerful study of the principles of Scripture and by their intelligent application to the case at hand."[74]

Prayer

Paul wrote to the Roman church, "In the same way, the Spirit helps us in our weakness. For we don't know what we ought to pray, but the Spirit himself intercedes for us with groaning that

---

74 J. Oswald Sanders, *Every Life Is a Plan of God: Discovering His Will for Your Life* (Grand Rapids, MI: Discovery House, 1992), 109.

words cannot express. And he who searches the heart knows what the mind of the Spirit is, because the Spirit intercedes for the saints according to the will of God" (Romans 8:26–27).

Prayer is talking and listening to God. God knows his will for our lives and wants us to know it, and for us to do it. As Henry Blackaby said, "What happens when you pray? The Holy Spirit knows what God already has waiting for you. His task is to get you to want it—to get you to ask for it."[75]

Prayer is a vehicle for increased faith. We sometimes live in the tension of not wanting to miss out on God's best for us while at the same time not wanting to do what we think God wants. Praying about what we should do brings courage and surrender. It is faith fortitude.

One day, Jesus was teaching his disciples life principles about temptation, causing others to stumble, and forgiveness. The disciples knew they were unable and probably did not want to heed Jesus's commands. They did have the presence of mind to ask the Lord for help: "Lord, increase our faith!" (Luke 17:1–5) was their request. And the Lord graciously complied.

Prayer also brings God's peace. Getting clarity on what God wants us to do can be stressful. Our minds can conjure up all kinds of worst-case scenarios. We need the comfort of prayer to calm us; Paul exhorted the Philippians to "be anxious for nothing, but in everything by prayer and supplication with thanksgiving let your requests be made known unto God. And the peace of God, which passes all understanding, shall guard your hearts and minds by Christ Jesus" (Philippians 4:6–7).

If we can't get peace, it is probably best to wait. As clergyman and author Phillips Brooks said, "Nothing lies beyond the reach of prayer except that which lies outside the will of God."[76]

---

75 Blackaby, 174
76 https://www.christianquotes.info/quotes-by-author/phillips-brooks-quotes/

Circumstances

Acts 17:27 states, "And [God] made from one man every nation of mankind to live on all the face of the earth, having determined allotted periods and the boundaries of their dwelling place, that they should seek God" (ESV).

God in his infinite wisdom caused us to be born in a certain place, at a certain time. Rich or poor, big or small, smart or not so smart, good looking or less good looking—these are the circumstances in which we find ourselves. This is not to suggest that we are locked into a preordained fate. By the grace of God, we can change our circumstances.

It is natural to seek to improve our conditions, and there is merit in the quest, especially when there is abuse or discontent. We should work toward desired outcomes. In such circumstances, seek God and work for positive change. After all, "to everything there is a season, and a time to every purpose under heaven" (Ecclesiastes 3:1).

There are also times when God will allow us to stay in difficult circumstances as part of his divine will. In such times, we should make the most of the situation and see it as an opportunity to grow and mature. If you can't get out of it, get into it!

When the apostle Paul was imprisoned, he prayed and sang songs at midnight (Acts 16:25). When John was exiled on the island of Patmos, God inspired him to write the book of Revelation. God puts us right where we are in order to glorify him. Trust his Providence. When the time is right, he will change the situation, change us, or tell us to change it. Until then, blossom where you are. Paul said, "In any and every circumstance, I have learned the secret of facing plenty and hunger, abundance and need. *I can do all things through him who strengthens me*" (Philippians 4:13; emphasis added).

Godly Counsel

Proverbs 15:22 advises, "Without counsel purposes are disappointed: but in the multitude of counselors they are established" (KJV).

Godly advice is a great resource in seeking the will of God. Trusted people can give us their life lessons, clarify vision, and encourage us. Many a believer can benefit from the wisdom of their pastor, deacon, or Christian friends who know and believe in us. Seek them out. Author and pastor Mark Corts said, "Test what you believe to be the will of God against the mind and heart of friends whom you respect in the Lord. Ask them to pray for direction. Be open to their counsel."[77]

Samuel was a boy serving in the temple of the Lord under the tutelage of Eli, the high priest. God spoke directly to Samuel, but Samuel was too young to understand God's voice. He thought Eli was speaking to him. When Samuel told Eli about the situation, the aged priest wisely perceived that God was speaking to the boy. Eli counseled him to listen to the voice, because it was the voice of God (1 Samuel 3).

When God is speaking to us, he will often give wisdom to others who can help us confirm God's direction. Don't be afraid to engage them in the conversation. In seeking the advice of godly people, a word of advice is key: godly counsel is helpful, but the decision is ours.

Guided Mind

God gave us a brain for thinking. Sometimes we can over-spiritualize a perceived prompting of the Lord when the better path is to think it through. The great Methodist minister and revivalist John Wesley said, "God generally guides me by

---

[77] C. Mark Corts, *The Caring Christian (Winston Salem, NC: Sharelife, 1990)*, 80

presenting reasons to my mind for acting a certain way."[78] Wise advice from a godly man. God's will is not opposed to great thinking.

One way we make great decisions is by asking great questions. Three questions can be used to facilitate any decision-making process.

First: "How does this glorify God?" God will not ask us to pursue a direction in which he cannot be glorified. As Paul said to the Corinthians, "Whether you eat or drink, do all for the glory of God" (1 Corinthians 10:31).

A second question should be "What effect does this have on others?" Will our decision build others up or put a stumbling block in someone else's path? Paul said, "Pursue what makes for peace and for building up one another" (Romans 14:19).

A third question to consider is "Does what I think God wants me to do fit with the way he has wired me?" God has given us gifts, talents, abilities, and temperament, among other things. He usually works in cooperation with the way he has made us. Don't get me wrong: God can call us to do anything he wants. And he may call us to do things we are not naturally good at in order to unleash talents and abilities we did not know we have. Be open to his leading as well as being mindful of how he has already equipped you to serve.

In discerning the will of God, due diligence is a wise path. Gather information about the decision to be considered. List the pros and cons. Think of a plan for what it will take to achieve the goal. Jesus spoke about the cost of discipleship that applies to God's will for our lives: "Which of you, intending to build a tower, does not first sit down and count the cost to see if he has enough to finish it?" (Luke 14:28).

---

[78] https://www.preceptaustin.org/the_will_of_god

COUNSEL FROM GODLY MEN WHO DISCOVERED GOD'S WILL

The following men are known for their walk with God and effectiveness in Christian ministry. Let's look at the criteria they developed for discerning God's will.

George Müller, *How to Ascertain the Will of God*[79]

I seek at the beginning to get my heart into such a state that it has no will of its own in regard to a given matter. Nine-tenths of the trouble with people generally is just here. Nine-tenths of the difficulties are overcome when our hearts are ready to do the Lord's will, whatever that may be. When one is truly in this state, it is usually but a little way to the knowledge of what His will is.

Having done this, I do not leave the result to feeling or simple impression. If so, I make myself liable to great delusions.

I seek the will of the Spirit of God through, or in connection with, the Word of God. The Spirit and the Word must be combined. If I look to the Spirit alone without the Word, I lay myself open to great delusions also. If the Holy Ghost guides us at all, He will do it according to the Scriptures and never contrary to them.

Next, I take into account providential circumstances. These often plainly indicate God's will in connection with His Word and Spirit.

I ask God in prayer to reveal His will to me aright.

Thus, through prayer to God, the study of the Word, and reflection, I come to a deliberate judgment according to the best of my ability and knowledge; and if my mind is thus at peace, and continues so after two or three more petitions, I proceed accordingly. In trivial matters, and in transactions involving the most important issues, I have found this method always effective.

---

[79] https://www.georgemuller.org/devotional/how-i-ascertain-the-will-of-god

Billy Graham

Below are Billy Graham's six guidelines on how we can discover God's will when we face a major decision:[80]

First, commit your decision to God. Make it a matter of regular prayer, asking God to guide you and make His will known to you.

Second, read the Scriptures. Does the Bible give any direct guidance about the decision you are facing? Does any principle in the Bible apply to your situation? Did anyone in the Bible ever face a similar decision, and, if so, how did they deal with it? (We can even learn from the wrong decisions some of them made.)

Third, understand your circumstances. God isn't only working in us; He also is working around us. Often God guides us through our circumstances.

Fourth, seek godly advice. God has given some people a special gift of wisdom, and when we face a decision, it's often helpful to seek their counsel.

Fifth, trust the Holy Spirit's guidance. When we honestly seek His will, God often gives us an inner conviction or prompting to confirm which way He wants us to go. The Bible says, "Whether you turn to the right or to the left, your ears will hear the voice behind you saying, 'This is the way; walk in it'" (Isaiah 30:21).

Finally, trust God for the outcome. Once God leads you to make a decision, don't draw back. Instead, trust His leading, and believe He goes before you—for He does. The Bible says, "Trust in the LORD with all your heart and lean not on your own understanding; in all your ways acknowledge Him and He will make your paths straight" (Proverbs 3:5–6).

---

80 https://billygrahamlibrary.org/6-steps-on-finding-gods-will/

Henry Blackaby

The following are Henry Blackaby's Seven Realities of experiencing God:[81]

- ◊ Reality One: God is always at work around you.
- ◊ Reality Two: God pursues a continuing love relationship with you that is real and personal.
- ◊ Reality Three: God invites you to become involved with him in his work.
- ◊ Reality Four: God speaks by the Holy Spirit through the Bible, prayer, circumstances, and the church to reveal himself, his purposes, and his ways.
- ◊ Reality Five: God's invitation for you to work with him always leads you to a crisis of belief that requires faith and action.
- ◊ Reality Six: You must make major adjustments in your life to join God in what he is doing.
- ◊ Reality Seven: You come to know God by experience as you obey him and he accomplishes his work through you.

CONCLUSION

Discovering the will of God for our lives is critical for being directed in the "all things" he wants us to do. It will empower us when we are "abased" and keep us humbly grateful when we "abound." The next chapter shows another aspect of the "all

---

[81] Henry Blackaby and Claude King, *Experiencing God: Knowing and Doing the Will of God* (Nashville: B&H Publishing Group, 2008).

things" God has for us in how he has wired us to achieve his will.

CAN DO; GO DO

Spend time in prayer asking God to reveal his will for your life.

What is God leading you to do? Go for it.

CHAPTER 16
SHAPE

We are uniquely designed by God to reach our God-given potential through Christ.

"Before I formed you in the womb I knew you, and before you were born I consecrated you; I appointed you a prophet to the nations."

JEREMIAH 1:5

"You were born by His purpose and for His purpose."

RICK WARREN

My family and I vacationed in the Smoky Mountains and drove to the Arts and Crafts Community in Gatlinburg, Tennessee. It is an eight-mile loop of over one hundred shops with artisans of all kinds: pottery, jewelry, basket weaving, candle making, sculpting, painting, metalworking, and many others. We did most of our Christmas shopping in one afternoon in July!

We purchased laser-engraved Christmas ornaments from the Wood Cottage and met the owner, Dave, and his little dog Finnegan. We also stopped in at one of the pottery shops to buy some handmade bowls. I stood and watched the potter at the wheel craft raw lumps of clay into cups, bowls, and vases. She used her hands to shape the earthly material from the bottom up, delicately transforming the pieces into beautiful and functional works of art.

The Bible describes God as the potter and humans as clay. He shapes our lives into something beautiful—if we cooperate. He has uniquely formed us to be and do what he has prepared for us (Ephesians 2:10). Evangelical author David Jeremiah reminds us, "The dominant theme in Scripture is a simple one: God is the Divine Potter and humanity is the clay. It is a way to express the picture of God's sovereignty over all people and to express our need to yield to his divine plan. It is a way to encourage us to find the purpose for which we have been made and to accept the divine purpose for all God's handiwork."[82]

This chapter will explore five aspects of our conditioning God uses to guide us in the "all things" we can achieve through Christ.[83]

FIVE ELEMENTS THAT SHAPE OUR LIVES

Have you ever wished you were someone else? I think we all have. What is so perplexing is that we often wish to be the opposite of what we are: extroverts wish they were introverts; shorter people want to be taller. We wish we were talented in areas in which we could never equal our current level of proficiency in other talents we do have. For example, Michael Jordan, one of the greatest basketball players of all time, wanted

---

82 https://davidjeremiah.blog/what-it-means-to-be-clay-in-the-hands-of-the-potter/

83 Some of the material of this chapter is adapted from Saddleback Church's Class 301: Discovering My SHAPE for Ministry.

to play baseball. He was not particularly successful.

Wanting to be someone else, or something else, can create a frustrating existence unless we realize God has made us with our own unique gifts, talents, tendencies, and life experiences. Before we were born, he predetermined some things. The other things come from our environment and life experiences. These forces are easily defined in the SHAPE acronym:

- ◇ Spiritual gifts
- ◇ Heart (passion)
- ◇ Abilities
- ◇ Personality
- ◇ Experiences

These are certainly not all of the components of life, but identifying these five characteristics will help us discover the unique ways God has made us. As a result, we can better assess the direction he would have us go. Let's look at each component individually.

Spiritual Gifts

What is a spiritual gift? A spiritual gift is a supernatural enabling given by God to each Christian for the purpose of helping others and building the body of Christ—his church. Every believer has at least one gift, and some may have more. The specific gifts are catalogued in Romans 12, 1 Corinthians 12, Ephesians 4, and 1 Peter 4.

How do we discover our spiritual gift(s)?

First of all, read the chapters in the Bible where the gifts are mentioned (see above). As you read, you will begin to resonate with certain gifts.

Second, pray and ask God to show you your gift; as James said, "You have not because you ask not" (James 4:2).

Believe that God has given you a gift and wants you to know what your gift is!

Third, ask someone who knows you and is familiar with the gifts what they think your gift may be. Trusted friends can often see what we may be blind to.

Four, start serving in your church. Spiritual gifts are something God will reveal to us while we are serving him. First Corinthians 12:4 explains, "There are different kinds of gifts, but the same Spirit, and there are different kinds of service, but the same Lord."

We learn by doing! As you serve, ask yourself two questions:

Is this fulfilling?

Is this bearing fruit?

A fifth way of discovering our spiritual gifts is by taking a spiritual gift inventory. You can take one for free online.[84] When taking the survey, remember that a spiritual gift test will measure our tendencies based on what we think or how we feel at the time. It is not absolute proof of our gifts. Use the other suggestions in this chapter as well to get a clearer picture of what your gift might be.

Our spiritual gifts are to be discovered and developed for the glory of God and in service to his kingdom. But these gifts do not only operate when we are in church. They are part of how God has made us and part of who we are. Our greatest success comes when we are operating out of our giftedness, both spiritual and otherwise. Don't neglect your gift(s)!

Heart

Proverbs 3:5 advises, "Trust in the Lord with all your heart,

---

[84] https://goexplorethebible.com/wp-content/uploads/2018/03/DOC-Spiritual-Gifts-Survey.pdf

and lean not on your own understanding. In all your ways acknowledge him, and he shall direct your path." Ephesians 6:6 speaks of "doing the will of God from the heart." And Psalms 37:4 says to "delight yourself in the Lord, and he will give you the desires of your heart" (ESV).

I have a friend who is an auto mechanic. He loves to work on cars. During the day, he is a wrench-turning motor head at the shop where he is employed. In the evenings, he works on his own hot rod. Sometimes, on weekends, he repairs vehicles for single moms who cannot afford to have their cars fixed or serviced. He sees his work as a calling. It is his passion.

What is your passion? A picture will start to form when we ask and answer the following questions:

- ◊ If I could do anything I want, and money were no object, what would I do?
- ◊ What do I think about?
- ◊ What keeps me up at night or gets me up in the morning?
- ◊ What problems would I like to solve?
- ◊ What cause would I like to be involved in?

These are questions of the heart. The answers to these questions may determine one's true passion.

God has given us inborn desires, interests, and motivations; these are part of our "heartbeat." Have you ever wondered why you like certain things but have no interest in others? Some people like arts and crafts, others sports. Some listen to pop music, while others prefer classical music. Some like the theater, while others like motocross. Some learn by reading, others by doing. One is not more right or wrong, just different. These qualities come from the way God has "shaped" us. Following our passions motivates us to pursue certain activities, interests, and environments. As we follow them, we find fulfillment and satisfaction in life.

In his book *S.H.A.P.E.: Finding and Fulfilling Your Unique Purpose In Life*, Eric Rees gives a list of clarifying questions to help discover our "heartbeat." I have adapted them and include them here.[85]

- ◇ What do I believe God wants me to do?
- ◇ What do my dreams and desires drift toward?
- ◇ What motivates me to take action?
- ◇ What do I care about?
- ◇ What needs do I like to meet?

Once we have asked some clarifying questions, the next step is to take action. We can do this by taking a course on a topic that interests us or getting involved in a ministry or cause that we feel passionate about. Having the heart to do something needs to be followed by learning how, and doing now! If not, the dream will probably die.

A word of caution to keep us from unbridled pursuit of whatever we think our hearts are telling us: "The heart is deceitful and above all things desperately wicked" (Jeremiah 17:9). Following our hearts should always draw us closer to God and in harmony with Scripture. Heart should also coordinate with the other components of our SHAPE. As author Rick Warren reminds us, "The Bible makes very clear that your heart was designed by God, but you make the choice to use it for good or evil, for selfish purposes or for service."[86]

---

[85] Erik E. Rees, *SHAPE* (Grand Rapids, MI: Zondervan, 2006).
[86] From Class 301: Discovering My SHAPE for Ministry.

Abilities

God told Moses to build the tabernacle in the wilderness. He gave him specific instructions on how the portable building was to look, what it should be made of, what furniture was to go inside, and who should build it. Moses was to supervise construction, but the responsibility of the actual building of the project was given to a man named Bezalel, and others who were gifted to work with their hands. As the Lord told Moses, "I have filled him [Bezalel] with the Spirit of God in wisdom, in understanding, in knowledge, and in all kinds of craftsmanship, to make artistic designs for work in gold, in silver, and in bronze, and in the cutting of stones for settings, and in the carving of wood, that he may work in all kinds of craftsmanship" (Exodus 31:3–5). Moses was a very able leader, but he needed the abilities of Bezalel to get the job done.

We have many talents and abilities—more than we think. Studies show that the average person may have as many as seven hundred abilities. Some abilities are basic, like walking and talking. Some others, like accounting or playing an instrument, are more complex and require time to develop. The key to a fulfilling life will consist of incorporating our abilities into our SHAPE.

Personality

My uncle Bobby was a free spirit; he did not want to be tied down to the "nine to five" work week. He enjoyed people and "shooting the breeze," generously offering his opinion about things that mattered to him. He wasn't averse to work but liked built-in flexibility. His temperament wasn't inclined toward rigid boundaries.

As a young man, Uncle Bobby worked in a mill, getting up every morning at the same time, going to the same place, operating the same machine in order to provide for his young family. The problem was Bobby was not suited for that kind of profession. It did not fit his "shape." He eventually switched careers and went into sales, where he was much more fulfilled and did well. Finding a vocation that fit his personality made all the difference in his life.

Compare him with my uncle John. He worked in a factory all of his adult life. For over thirty years, John went through the same door of the same building of the same company to the same work area to supervise the production of the same product. His personality was geared toward regularity and predictability.

Neither uncle was wrong in their career choice. Nor was one uncle "better" than the other. Each knew what suited him best, and both were wise enough to follow a path best fit for them. It takes all kinds to make the world work.

People have certain natural tendencies that derive from personality. Some are more introverted: they would rather be in the background. Others are more extroverted: they like to be in the forefront. Some are more nurturing, while others are more concerned with getting a task done. Neither is right or wrong; it's just the way we are wired.

Much study has been done in the area of temperament. Many companies and organizations use assessment tools such as DISC or the Myers–Briggs or Enneagram test to measure a person's personality and behavioral type. The thought behind such a tool is that people have predominant personality styles, and if a company can place a person in a position that best fits the individual's style, they will be more productive and fulfilled. The company will benefit because employees get more done when performing a job or task that is suited to the way they are wired.

A personality test can be a beneficial tool for helping understand how our unique personalities can help us better serve God. Certain tendencies lend themselves to fruitful service in certain areas and not in others. For instance, an introvert with the gift of helps should probably prepare the Sunday bulletin, while an extrovert with the gift of helps would be better suited to handing out the bulletin and talking to people as they enter the church building.

Knowing our personalities can also help us relate to people with different temperaments from ours. Sometimes we get frustrated when people do things differently from how we would. Think of two people putting together a puzzle. The "big picture" thinker wants to gather all the end pieces and establish borders, then work on the inside. The more detail-oriented thinker may see a part of the puzzle that interests them and look for those particular pieces. Both are needed for all of the puzzle pieces to get into the right place. When we are aware of different personalities, we can appreciate that God has given another individual a different approach to tackling tasks instead of becoming frustrated.

There are benefits to exploring how God has shaped us through our personalities, but there are also some things to keep in mind. First, our true identity is in Christ, not a personality test. As Paul directed the Colossians, "Set your mind on things above, not on earthly things. For you died, and your life is now hidden with Christ in God" (Colossians 3:2–3).

Second, personality has been affected by sin and can be used to hurt, sometimes unwittingly. For instance, someone with a dominant personality can overpower more cooperative types in order to get their own way. Their motives may be pure, but their tactics seem harsh. Our personalities must come under the lordship of Christ and be renewed by the Holy Spirit. As Paul wrote to the Corinthians, "And we all, with unveiled face, beholding the glory of the Lord, are being transformed into the same image from one degree of glory to another. For this comes from the Lord who is the Spirit" (2 Corinthians 3:18 ESV).

Experiences

One of the most overlooked factors in determining our life shapes is our past experiences, both positive and negative. Victories as well as trials and tribulations are part of living but not always part of our learning. By the grace of God, we have overcome difficulties, hurts, and hang-ups. They are part of our life stories—our education from the "school of hard knocks." We are experts in our life experiences!

We can discover insight into our life shapes by considering the following experiences:

- ◇ Educational experiences: What were your favorite subjects in school? What kind of formal training have you had?

- ◇ Vocational experiences: What jobs have you enjoyed and achieved results while doing?

- ◇ Spiritual experiences: What meaningful and decisive experiences have you had with God?

- ◇ Relational experiences: How have you learned to love people? How have you served others? How have you handled difficult relationships?

- ◇ Ministry experiences: How and in what capacity have you served God in the past? Was it fulfilling? Was it fruitful?

- ◇ Painful experiences: Never waste a hurt, because sharing the story of your pain can lessen the hurt of someone else's. It seems more comforting to cry on the shoulder of someone who has shed the same tears. God allows us to experience difficulty so we can "be of comfort" to others when they are going through difficult times (2 Corinthians 1:4). What are the problems, hurts, and trials that you have experienced in life? What have you learned from them?

How can you take what you have experienced and help others who are enduring similar things? Take the lessons you have learned from the difficulties of life and gift them to someone else.

Spiritual gifts, heart, abilities, personality, and experiences are keys to unlocking the "all things" God has in store for us. Reflect on them, pray over them, and act on them. God will bless our endeavors.

CONCLUSION

God has given shape to our lives. Some of it predetermined, while other dimensions have been developed by our environments and experiences. A key aspect of success is to discover how God has shaped us and harness the knowledge to pursue our God-given dreams for his glory and reach our full potential in Christ.

Some people will try to negate our dreams instead of nurturing them. In *Success* magazine, author and former publisher Darren Hardy told a story of the eagle and the chickens:

On a large, majestic mountainside rested a fragile eagle's nest with four large eagle eggs. One day, an earthquake rocked the mountainside, causing one of the eagle's eggs to tumble down the mountain to a chicken farm located in the valley below. A mother hen found the egg and knew instinctively she must protect it, so she volunteered to nurture the large egg.

One day, the egg hatched, and a beautiful eagle was born. But the eagle was raised to be a chicken. His chicken environment led him to believe he was a chicken. He loved his home and family, but his heart cried out for more. While playing a game on the farm with some of the other chickens, the eagle looked up in the sky above and noticed a group of mighty eagles soaring above.

"Oh," said the eagle, "I wish I could soar like those birds."

The chickens laughed, "You can't soar with those birds. You are a chicken, and chickens don't soar."

The eagle continued staring at his unknown family in the sky, dreaming he would be one of them. Each time the eagle shared his dreams with his chicken family, he was told it could not be done. The eagle eventually stopped dreaming and continued to live his life as a chicken. Finally, after a long life as a chicken, the eagle died—as a chicken.

Don't die a chicken. Have the courage to find and develop your SHAPE. Take time to discover how God has made you. Follow your God-inspired heart and soar like an eagle!

CAN DO; GO DO

- ◇ Take a spiritual gift assessment. One can be found at https://goexplorethebible.com/wp-content/uploads/2018/03/DOC-Spiritual-Gifts-Survey.pdf. Remember, it is a helpful tool, but the results are not written in stone.

- ◇ Take a personality test to discover some of your personality strengths. DISC, the Myers–Briggs, or Enneagram tests can be found online.

SECTION 6

"THROUGH CHRIST"

The Christian life is lived out by the power of Christ living in us. Achievement comes by Christ doing his work through us.

"I can do all things **through Christ** who strengthens me."

CHAPTER 17
ABIDING IN CHRIST

We are connected to Christ. As we walk close with him, he does his work in us and through us.

"I am the vine, you are the branches, he that abides in me and I in him will bear much fruit, for apart from me you can do nothing."

JOHN 15:5

"You are the branches of the Lord Jesus Christ. If there is in your heart the consciousness that you are not a strong, healthy, fruit-bearing branch, not closely linked with Jesus, not living in Him as you should be—then listen to Him say: 'I am the Vine, I will receive you, I will draw you to myself, I will bless you, I will strengthen you, I will fill you with my Spirit.'"

ANDREW MURRAY, *ABSOLUTE SURRENDER*

We are saved by Christ. We live for Christ. In heaven, we will be with Christ. We give praise, thanks, and glory to Christ. We depend on Christ. We are in the service of Christ.

Jesus gave his followers a commanding truth: he will do the work through us as we walk with him in a loving-obedient relationship. Developing as a disciple of Christ means living out God's will for our lives while pursuing our God-given dreams and goals—doing the will of God by the power of God for the glory of God. Success is a by-product of Christ living in us and doing his work through us.

In the Gospel of John chapter 15, our Lord uses the imagery of a vine to tell a story about living a productive Christian life. The secret is to stay connected to him. Just as the branch of a grapevine has to stay connected to the main vine in order to live and produce fruit, the believer's connection to the Savior allows us to live a fruitful life. How can we abide in Christ?

LIVING IN HIS PRESENCE

There is no hard-and-fast recipe for abiding in Christ: two parts Bible, one part prayer, and a pinch of obedience baked into the Christian life will not result in a dish known as "abiding." Abiding is more of an awareness that, day by day, we are in the presence of God and surrendered to his plan and purpose for our life. It is a conscious desire to walk with him obediently. It is also conviction that God promises his power to work in us to accomplish his plan. As such, we can live in peace and experience his power because our strength and sustenance come from Jesus.

Though no recipe will guarantee "abiding," the following practices will facilitate living in the presence and experiencing the power of Christ in our lives.

Realizing that Christ Is the Source of Life and Success

Jesus declared, "I am the vine, my father is the vinedresser" (John 15:1).

There may be many contributing factors to a person's

success; hard work, privilege, courage, intellect, talent, and relationships come to mind. But where do those tools for success come from? What is the source that gives direction, desire, drive, and self-denial in pursuing our dreams? For the believer, it comes from God the Son! As Paul explained to the Galatians, "I have been crucified with Christ, and it is no longer I who live but Christ who lives in me. And the life I live in the flesh I live by faith in the Son of God, who loved me and delivered himself up for me" (Galatians 2:20).

Realizing Christ is the source of all success reinforces God's promise to empower us and reminds us of our need to walk close to him.

George Washington Carver was born a slave and grew up without a father or mother, yet God used him to bless the world. Carver established the agricultural school at Tuskegee Institute in Alabama. Through his research he discovered over three hundred uses of peanuts. Carver believed the source of his knowledge came from God: "God is going to reveal to us things he never revealed before if we put our hands in his."[87] God still has many advances in science and technology to reveal to people who seek him as the source of all things worth knowing and doing.

Receiving Christ as Savior and Lord

Abiding in Christ begins when we receive Christ as Savior and Lord: "But as many as received him, to them he gave the right to become children of God, even to those who call upon his name" (John 1:2).

It all starts when we come to faith in Jesus though repentance of sin and call on him to save us from our deficient selves and declare his lordship over our lives. If you have not yet come to faith in Christ, re-read chapter 11 and call on him as Savior and Lord.

---

87 https://everydaypower.com/george-washington-carver-quotes/

Releasing Ourselves to Christ

First Peter 5:6–7 exhorts Christians, "Humble yourselves, therefore, under God's mighty hand, that he may lift you up in due time. Cast all your cares upon him because he cares for you."

The Christian life has been called the "exchanged life." We exchange our sin for God's salvation, our inability for his ability, our lack for God's abundance and provision.

The exchanged life is experienced not by thinking we have to hold on to Christ but by trusting he will never let go of us. Bill Bright, the founder of Campus Crusade for Christ, said, "This is the way I live moment by moment: Christ in me. I am just a suit of clothes for Him. By faith, I have exchanged my own life of failures and defeats for His life of victory, love and joy."[88]

When someone flies on an airplane, the only thing they have to do to get to their destination is get on the plane and stay in the plane until it lands. While on the plane, they are free to work, eat, sleep, read, talk, and do anything else allowed within the confines of the plane. Life is like taking a plane ride, with Jesus as the plane maker and pilot who has a perfect flying record. We get to our destination with him, by him, and because of him.

Releasing oneself to Christ involves the conscious awareness that we are putting him in charge and trusting him. We relinquish our imperfect human control to his perfect will. This shift can be expressed by a simple yet powerful prayer of faith:

> Heavenly Father, in Jesus' name I release myself to you. I surrender my strengths and abilities to you. I also give you my inability and lack in exchange for your abundant power and provision. Lord Jesus abide in me and I in you. For without you I can do nothing. Amen.

---

88 https://www.crosswalk.com/devotionals/insights-from-bill-bright/the-exchanged-life-dec-26.html

Remaining in Fellowship with Him

To abide means "to remain, to stay connected to." Think of a lamp. As long as the switch is on and the cord is connected to the electricity supplied to the wall socket, power flows to the light bulb. When the cord is disconnected, the light goes out immediately because the electrical power has been cut. The switch may still be on, but power comes from the source, not the switch.

Loving obedience is the cord that keeps the power of Christ flowing to us. He said, "If you keep my commandments, you will abide in my love" (John 15:10).

Obedience may sound demeaning to our culture. Some would say it is what we train dogs to demonstrate. Such a belief is far from the notion of obedience as promoted in Scripture. Doing what Jesus says keeps us closely connected to him and gives us joy. Disobedience causes a disconnect between the believer and Jesus, which brings frustration and anxiety.

Jesus compared abiding in him to a branch staying connected to a vine: "Abide in me and I in you. As the branch cannot bear fruit of itself, unless it abides in the vine, neither can you, unless you abide in me" (John 15:4). A fruitful branch has to stay connected to the nutrients provided by the vine.

Our daughter came home from college break, and we went on a walk together. It was great to get reacquainted after she had been gone for the semester. We walked along a path at the state park, talking about her school and my work. She wanted to know how my book was progressing and what I thought about our country's current political climate. We stopped along the way and looked at a rendition of an original Native American hut. We were in fellowship. It was a great afternoon.

As I think about our walk, I realize we incorporated the principles of abiding: First, we were going in the same direction. Second, we talked to one another. Third, we wanted to know each other's thoughts and ideas. Fourth, we shared the same activities. The ties that bind us closer to Jesus are tightened when we walk in the direction he is going, talk with him through prayer, listen to him in Scripture, and obediently serve him.

Responding to His Pruning

Jesus explains of God, "Every branch that bears fruit he prunes, that it may bear more fruit" (John 15:2).

Shoots on a grapevine have to be pruned yearly in order to maintain vine form and maximize healthy fruit yield. It takes a skilled gardener to cut off the right amount of branches without damaging the plant.

Abiding in Christ involves God "pruning" away the things in our lives that keep us from reaching our God-given potential in Christ. God's pruning in our life is good; it's used to shape us into the image of Christ. It is a "discipline of discipleship." It can be painful, but God will cause it to work together for good. In pruning, God is cutting away the things that will prove to be unproductive. These things may or may not be sinful in themselves. What we need to remember is they are an impediment to abiding in Christ.

Pruning can make us bitter or better, depending on how we respond. If we see pruning as loss and punishment from God, we will miss the blessing. If we use the pruning process to draw nearer to Christ for comfort and help, we will tap into the eternal resources of God.

Don't just go through the pruning; *grow* through it!

Resting in His Love

"As the Father loved me, I also have loved you; abide in my love," Jesus told his disciples (John 15:9).

The key to abiding in Christ is to realize we are truly loved by God and can rest in his promise that he will never leave us nor forsake us. Our relationship with him is not a competition to win his approval. Nor is it a contest to see how few sins we commit. If we receive Christ as Savior and Lord, he has done all of the work to procure a right standing for us before the Father. Rest on his outstretched arms that hung on the cross.

THE EXCHANGED LIFE

J. Hudson Taylor spent fifty years as a missionary to China and was the founder of the China Inland Mission. He was known for his tireless efforts in reaching the Chinese with the gospel and recruiting missionaries for service. Over the course of his ministry, Taylor evangelized the Chinese, recruited hundreds of missionaries, started schools and medical clinics, translated parts of the Bible into Chinese, worked as a medical practitioner, and traveled to Britain, Canada, Australia, the United States, and other parts of the world to speak of the need to reach China with the gospel. Outwardly, he did not seem to have an "off" button!

His life was also marked with hardship and personal tragedy. Hudson was often in ill health and suffered bouts of depression. He was paralyzed for several months due to a fall. He went through financially lean periods. His leadership style was criticized by fellow missionaries as autocratic. His first wife, Maria, died at age thirty-three, and four of their children died before reaching the age of ten.

Hudson Taylor lived a life devoted to God. Yet he went through periods of spiritual dryness. He thought the answer was to work harder to be holy and do more work in reaching the Chinese for Christ. So he prayed more, fasted, and strove to do better. But the harder he worked, the more he despaired—bemoaning his sin, yet feeling powerless to overcome. He was fretful and anxious, and experienced little joy.

When his "agony of soul" was at its worst, Taylor remembered a quote from a letter sent to him by his friend John McCarthy: "But how to get faith strengthened? Not by striving after faith, but by resting on the Faithful One." Like a light had been turned on, Taylor realized he must "exchange" the work he was doing in his own strength for the power of Christ working through him. He understood the unlimited power available to him by abiding in Christ: "The vine now I see, is not the root merely, but all—root, stem, branches, twigs, leaves, flowers, fruit: and Jesus is not only that: He is soil and sunshine, air and showers, and ten thousand times more than we have ever dreamed, wished for, or needed."[89]

After his epiphany of abiding in Christ, Taylor's circumstances did not change. He still worked hard, faced difficulties, prayed, and served. The difference was that he went about his life and tasks with the release of anxiety because he was resting in Christ. He lived with the calm assurance that he no longer lived in his own power, but rather Christ lived in him.

CONCLUSION

Abiding in Christ is supernatural. It is something we do not strive for but instead release ourselves to. Being in Christ happens the moment we believe in him for salvation. Abiding in Christ is the conscious awareness that all things come when we release ourselves to Jesus who is living in and working through us. The conscious awareness of abiding in Christ can take time. We have to grow into it.

Give yourself time, and pray for greater awareness that you are indeed connected to Christ and greater works you will do, because he has gone to the Father (John 14:12).

---

89 https://www.wholesomewords.org/missions/biotaylor11.html

CAN DO; GO DO

◇ Look over the suggested prayer in this chapter for abiding in Christ, and pray it in faith, from the heart.

◇ What act of loving obedience will you complete today through the power of Christ within you?

CHAPTER 18
LIVING WATER

The Holy Spirit lives in every believer to empower us to serve and reach our God-given potential in Christ.

"The grace of the Lord Jesus Christ, and the love of God, and the communion of the Holy Spirit, be with you all. Amen."

1 CORINTHIANS 13:14

"Therefore in our Christian lives it is important that we depend on the Holy Spirit's power, recognizing that any significant work is done 'Not by might, nor by power, but by my Spirit, says the LORD of hosts' (Zech. 4:6)."

WAYNE GRUDEM

High up in the snow-clad peaks of the Andes Mountains, ice begins to melt and form pools of water. The water trickles down the hillsides. The flow increases as multiple streams of water converge into the world's largest river, the Amazon. The river is over four thousand miles long and curves through the tropical rain forests and dense vegetation of nine South American countries. During the rainy season, it can reach widths of almost twenty-five miles and depths of over three hundred feet.

The river is the fount of life for thousands of species of fish and other wildlife. The Amazon deposits fifty-eight million gallons of water per second into the Atlantic, roughly the equivalent of eighty-eight Olympic-sized swimming pools. It comprises about 20 percent of the ocean's fresh water supply. Plumes of fresh water can be detected up to one hundred miles into the Atlantic Ocean's salt water.[90] From almost undetectable sources of water comes an unstoppable power that provides life to all that drink from it.

WHO IS THE HOLY SPIRIT?

Before Jesus physically left the earth, he promised the disciples he would send a helper to live in them and enable them to serve him and live a God-honoring life. This helper is the Holy Spirit. He is the unseen source that brings rivers of God's unstoppable power to converge in the believer's life.

The Holy Spirit is God and the third person of the Trinity. Our minds are not great enough to grasp the magnificence and complexity of God. We must accept the nature of God by faith, based on how he is revealed in the Old and New Testaments of the Bible.

All of the attributes of deity are possessed by the Holy Spirit. He is eternal (Hebrews 9:14), omnipresent (Psalms 139:7–10), all knowing (1 Corinthians 2:10–11), and all powerful (Luke 1:35–37). He was active at the creation of the universe (Genesis 1:1–2). Jesus was raised from the dead by the power of the Spirit (Romans 1:4). The Holy Spirit inspired the human writers of Holy Scripture (2 Peter 1:20–21). He is also active in the world today (John 16:8).

---

[90] www.earthobservatory.nasa.gov

The Holy Spirit is not an impersonal force. Nor is he a personal "unseen" something that brings us good luck when we are good. He cannot be conjured up like a genie when a person needs extra power.

There is one living and true God. He is the all-knowing and all-powerful Creator and sustainer of the universe. The one God is triune, eternally existing as Father, Son, and Holy Spirit. These three Persons are distinct in personal attributes yet equally God and of the same essence and being.

How do we understand the relationship between God the Father, God the Son, and God the Holy Spirit? Any attempt to fully explain the complete nature of God would not fully express the grandeur of his essence. John 15:26 tells us the Holy Spirit "proceeds from the Father and [is] sent by the Son." Like the nature of the Trinity itself, we accept it by faith, realizing there are certain aspects of the nature of God we will not fully comprehend in this life. As Moses conveyed to the people of Israel, "the secret things belong to the Lord" (Deuteronomy 29:29).

THE HOLY SPIRIT WORKS IN US

We have established that the Holy Spirit is the third person of the Trinity of God. But what does he do? More specifically, what role does the Holy Spirit play in the life of the Christian? The following tenets will provide better understanding on how the Holy Spirit works in the believer's life.

The Holy Spirit Helps the Believer

Jesus said, "And I will ask the Father, and he will give you another Helper [Advocate, Counselor], to be with you forever, even the Spirit of truth" (John 14:16,17a).

The term "helper" refers to someone who comes alongside another. In a legal sense, it is one who advocates for the defense against accusations from an accuser. In the broadest sense, it refers to someone who helps in times of need, whatever the need may be. The same synonym provided above is used to describe Jesus in 1 John 2:1: "And if anyone sins, we have an Advocate with the Father, Jesus Christ the righteous."

We all need help! As minister Lloyd John Ogilvie said, "Life 'de-powers' us. It saps our energies, depletes our courage, drains our patience. People-pressures get us down; problems stir us up; physical ills distress us; worry over people we love disturbs us. We all need strength—strength to think clearly, love creatively, endure consistently; strength to fill up our diminished reserves; supernatural strength that flows from a limitless source, quietly filling us with power."[91] Thanks be to God he gives us help! On our own, we cannot think right, do right, or live right—at least, right enough. We need God's abundant grace through the power of the Holy Spirit.

The Holy Spirit Empowers the Believer

In Acts 1:8, Jesus says, "You shall receive power when the Holy Spirit has come upon you; and you shall be my witnesses in Jerusalem, Judea and Samaria, and to the utmost parts of the earth."

In addition to being our helper, the Holy Spirit gives us his power! As helper, the Holy Spirit comes to our aid. As the one who empowers, the Holy Spirit enables us to stand up and stand out as "witness" to people who are watching.

What does it mean to be a "witness" for Jesus? Our witness refers to the words we use and the way we live as we present ourselves to the world as followers of Christ. Effective witness can only be achieved through God's power. As theologian J. I.

---

[91] Lloyd John Ogilvie sermon "Two Thirds Is Not Enough"

Packer tells us, "We are called to fight evil in all its forms in and around us, and we need to learn that in this battle the Spirit's power alone gives victory, while self-reliance leads only to the discovery of one's impotence and the experience of defeat."[92] As Christians, we have the Holy Spirit, who resources us to live in God's infinite power.

One of the ways the Spirit empowers us is through spiritual gifts: "To each one of us a manifestation of the Spirit is given for the good of all" (1 Corinthians 12:7). As mentioned in the SHAPE chapter, the Holy Spirit has gifted each of us with at least one spiritual gift. It is to be used to serve people as a witness for Christ. Operating in our giftedness is the "sweet spot" for life and service.

The Spirit also empowers us to be virtuous. As Galatians 5:22 says, "Now the fruit of the Spirit is love, joy, peace, patience, kindness, goodness, gentleness, faithfulness, self-control; against such things there is no law."

The Holy Spirit transforms our nature. By his power working through us, he supernaturally renews our attitudes and actions. As we live under his control, we become better people and reflect the image of Christ. Pastor Charles Swindoll said,

> What fuel is to a car, the Holy Spirit is to the believer. He energizes us to stay the course. He motivates us in spite of obstacles. He keeps us going when the road gets rough. It is the Spirit who comforts us in our distress, who calms us in time of calamity, who becomes our companion in loneliness and grief, who spurs our "intuition" into action, who fills our minds with discernment when we are uneasy about a certain decision. He is, in short, spiritual fuel.[93]

---

[92] https://www.cslewisinstitute.org/Power_From_Keep_In_Step_With_The_Spirit

[93] https://www.crosswalk.com/devotionals/todays-insight-chuck-swindoll/today-s-insight-july-4-2013.html

When a person comes to saving faith in Christ, they are immediately given a right standing before God. The sinner is declared righteous by God based on the perfect obedience of Jesus Christ in sacrificing himself on the cross as atonement for sin (2 Corinthians 5:21). This is a legal description of God's act of salvation. The theological term to describe this is "justification."

Sanctification refers more to the lifelong process of God changing our character to reflect the image and nature of Christ (Romans 8:29). At salvation, the believer is set apart or "sanctified" to God. In sanctification, the Holy Spirit is at work to make us "holy" in our character and conduct. He empowers us to live a life that is pleasing to God and make a difference in the world by bearing spiritual fruit.

Paul's prayer for the church at Ephesus was that God would strengthen them with power through his Spirit in the inner man (Ephesians 3:16). Every believer needs courage, character, fortitude, moral fiber, and mental toughness to reach their God-given potential in Christ. It is not a self-generated power. Man's inner strength comes from depending on the enabling power of the Holy Spirit. Pray for it and act like it.

The Holy Spirit Glorifies Christ

Jesus said, "He will glorify me, for he will take what is mine and show it to you" (John 16:14).

Many verses in the Bible speak of the Holy Spirit's work: he convicts people of sin (John 16:8), empowers believers to witness (Acts 1:8), imparts spiritual gifts to believers (1 Corinthians 12), and helps us pray (Romans 8:26), to name a few aspects. For all of his power to help us in our personal life, the role of the Spirit is to constantly draw our attention back to the greatness of the cross and resurrection of Jesus our Savior. The power of the Holy Spirit within us is only possible because of what Christ has done for us in saving us from our sin and making us right with God.

The Holy Spirit Guides the Believer

"When the Spirit of truth comes, he will guide you into all the truth, for he will not speak on his own authority, but whatever he hears he will speak, and he will declare to you the things that are to come," Jesus told his disciples in John 16:13 (ESV).

It is both comforting and empowering to know God still speaks to us today through his Holy Spirit.

We live in a world of information overload. According to Harris Andrea in an article for Tech 21 Century, a study conducted by researchers at the University of California–San Diego suggests people are inundated daily with thirty-four gigabytes or more of information. That's enough information to overload a laptop computer in a week! Harris says, "Through mobile phones, online entertainment services, the Internet, electronic mail, television, radio, newspapers, books, social media, etc., people receive every day about 105,000 words or 23 words per second in half a day (12 hours during awake hours)."[94]

Information does not equal guidance. Too much exposure to disparate information can cause loss of focus and lack of discernment. How do we know the information is true? How does the information integrate with a Christian worldview? How do we get the wisdom to understand how the information can help us reach our God-given potential through Christ? We need the guidance of the Holy Spirit to help us.

The Holy Spirit's primary means of guiding us into truth is the Bible. That is one reason why it is essential to be a student of Scripture. The devil wants to deceive us. The world wants to distract us from seeking God. Our own minds and hearts can dilute our understanding of God's will. We need something greater than ourselves to tell us the truth: God's Word. We also need someone to rightly interpret the truth and guide us

---

94 https://www.tech21century.com/the-human-brain-is-loaded-daily-with-34-gb-of-information

to apply it: God's Spirit. The Spirit will never tell us to disobey God's truth. That is why we can depend on both Scripture and the Spirit to lead us in the way everlasting.

Our minds can be fickle and flawed. We sometimes find it hard to know what to decide and then question ourselves once a decision is made. How do we discern what's true and false, what is good and what is best, what God wants and what we want? How can we have confidence in the daily decisions we make? God promises to guide us in life through the Holy Spirit illuminating the truth of God's Word and applying it to our specific situations. We may not always get it 100 percent right, but he is never wrong.

We hear the Spirit more clearly when we are abiding in Christ and walking close to the Lord with open hearts and renewed minds. Think of your favorite radio station. It has a broadcast range of about forty miles. Farther away from the signal, the channel becomes less clear. The signal can also be blocked by mountains and large buildings. The sound fades and is drowned out by static. The guidance of the Spirit is similar to a radio frequency in this way: the closer we walk with God, the clearer we hear his voice. When we avoid the mountains of sin and disobedience, we are in a better position to receive the guidance of the Holy Spirit.

The Holy Spirit Indwells Every Believer

Paul wrote the Corinthians, "Or do you not know that your body is a temple of the Holy Spirit within you, whom you have from God? You are not your own" (1 Corinthians 6:19 ESV).

To the Romans he declared, "You, however, are not in the flesh but in the Spirit, if indeed the Spirit of God dwells in you. But if anyone does not have the Spirit of Christ, he does not belong to him" (Romans 8:9).

At the moment of salvation, the believer is born into the

family of God (John 3:3) and baptized into the body of Christ (1 Corinthians 12:13), the seal of God's ownership is placed on them (Ephesians 1:13), and our place in heaven is guaranteed (Ephesians 1:14). All of these blessings are the result of the Holy Spirit coming to live in us—or indwelling us.

Yes, the Holy Spirit lives inside us! He will always be with us and equip us to do all the things God calls us to do. As we depend on him and live under his control, we will be directed, protected, and empowered.

BE FILLED WITH THE SPIRIT

In addition to indwelling every believer, God tells us to be filled with the Spirit: "Be not drunk with wine, which leads to excess, but be filled with the Spirit" (Ephesians 5:18).

There is a difference between the two events. The indwelling of the Spirit is a one-time event that happens at the moment of salvation. The Holy Spirit enters the new believer forever. The filling of the Holy Spirit is something that happens repeatedly as we call upon him for power and live under his direction and control. How can we be filled with the Spirit?

Have a Deep Desire for God

The purpose of being filled with the Spirit is to have a deeper love for Christ and a more fulfilling Christian walk. Some might think the Holy Spirit is like a spiritual power crystal one can win by reaching a higher level in a video game. The crystal is used to wield more power and get the player out of a jam when needed.

Not so with the Holy Spirit. He is not a game or toy that can be manipulated! Just the opposite is true. We don't control the Holy Spirit. He controls us. Being filled with the Spirit is born from a deeper thirst for God and a desire to experience him in deeper ways than merely getting what we want.

Confess and Repent of All Known Sin

First John 1:8–9 says, "If we say we have no sin, we are deceiving ourselves and the truth is not in us. If we confess our sin, He is faithful and just to forgive our sin and cleanse us from all unrighteousness."

The moment we are saved, we receive eternal cleansing and forgiveness for sin because Jesus took our punishment on the cross. Salvation does not depend on what we do for God. It is the result of what Jesus *has done* for us by dying for our sins and rising from the grave. Salvation is made secure by Jesus's promise and ability to never let us go (John 10:28).

Though we have been forgiven for sin, we still find ourselves committing sins. This may not be the believer's desire, but it is our reality. Sin is like holes in the bucket of life, causing the water of the Spirit to leak out. Thankfully, we do not have to be "re-saved" when we sin, but we do need to be restored to a closer walk with God. How is the relationship restored? By confessing our sins and repenting of them.

Confession means to agree with God that our attitudes and actions are against his will and are indeed sinful. The process involves admitting the wrongs we do to him as we specifically remember them. Repentance means to change our minds and hearts as well as our actions in regards to sins being committed. As Proverbs 28:13 advises, "He that covers his sin will not prosper, but whosoever confesses and forsakes them will find mercy."

In its truest form, repentance is turning away from sinful actions as well as from the desire that entices us to commit them.

Sin dirties our lives as well as the heart. It dulls our spiritual ears to the voice of God and disempowers our efforts to do the work of God. It also keeps us from reaching our God-given dreams and goals. Confession is like a spiritual scrub brush that cleans off the sinful dirt and restores the luster of a tarnished heart. "Admitting and quitting" are the keys of confession and repentance.

Take a moment and pray. Ask God to show you any sin or situation that inhibits his filling you with himself. Confess any sins that come to mind and turn from them. Think about your attitudes and actions today. Are you guilty of anger, greed, envy, lust, laziness, pride, or gluttony? Admit them to God, and thank him for forgiving you. Ask God to reveal anything that is offensive to him and lead you in the right way (Psalms 139:24).

Surrender Ourselves Afresh to God

Jesus said, "If anyone would come after me, let him deny himself daily and pick up his cross and follow me" (Luke 9:23). Being filled with the Spirit does not mean we have more of the Holy Spirit. It means the Holy Spirit has more of us. He is in control. Daily surrender to God's will and God's work will bring God's filling.

The great evangelist D. L. Moody said, "I firmly believe that the moment our hearts are emptied of selfishness and ambition and self-seeking and everything that is contrary to God's law, the Holy Spirit will come and fill every corner of our hearts; but if we are full of pride and conceit, ambition and self-seeking, pleasure and the world, there is no room for the Spirit of God."[95]

Pray. Ask God to provide the grace to empty yourself of the sinful self and fill you with himself.

Trust God and Obey

The Holy Spirit responds to an obedient life. The small streams of obedience will turn into a mighty river of the Holy Spirit's power, presence, and purpose in our lives.

---

95   https://www.azquotes.com/quote/1072564

Many years ago, a young man was asked to speak in a Christian meeting about what he would do as a follower of Christ. His reply: "I'm not quite sure, but I am going to trust, and I am going to obey." The incident was told to Reverend John Sammis, who used the words in the hymn "Trust and Obey": "When we walk with the Lord, in the light of his Word, what a glory He sheds on our way; when we do His good will, He abides with us still, and with all who will trust and obey. Trust and obey, for there's no other way to be happy in Jesus, but to trust and obey."[96]

As a first-year college student, theologian Wayne Grudem heard some teaching on the fullness of the Holy Spirit. The speaker exhorted the members of the audience to repent of all known sin and yield every area of their lives to God. As instructed, Grudem listened and complied. Using different vocabulary, but with the same understanding, he asked Jesus to fill him with the Holy Spirit. In his own words: "The result in my life was undoubtedly a positive and lasting one, including a much deeper love for Christ and much greater effectiveness in personal ministry."[97] The same can happen to us when we trust and obey.

WALK BY THE SPIRIT

Paul wrote the Galatians, "If we live by the Spirit, let us also walk by the Spirit" (Galatians 5:25).

When we are filled with the Spirit, we will walk by the Spirit. We have the life of God within us. We are not alone and are not to attempt to do it on our own. "Walk by the Spirit" derives

---

96 https://www.umcdiscipleship.org/resources/history-of-hymns-trust-and-obey

97 Wayne Grudem, *Systematic Theology* (Grand Rapids, MI: Zondervan, 1994), 765.

its meaning from a military term to walk in a straight line and keep pace like a soldier in formation. We are to walk the straight line of serving God and keeping pace with his Spirit. To live by the Spirit means we are continually living under his guidance, power, and control.

Much like abiding in Christ, walking in the Spirit means we are depending on God to work in us and accomplish his work through us. We are following the strong godly desires he creates in us and saying no to fleshly desires that hurt us. As Zechariah 4:6 says, "Not by might, nor by power, but by my Spirit says the Lord."

CONCLUSION

As we abide in Christ and live by the power of the Holy Spirit, we will see God work through us. Abiding in Christ allows us to rest in the results of God working on our behalf. Walking in the power of the Holy Spirit creates the energy to strive toward our God-given dreams and goals. Paul explained to the Corinthians, "Not that we are sufficient in ourselves, to claim anything is coming from ourselves, but our sufficiency is from God" (2 Corinthians 3:5 ESV).

CAN DO; GO DO

- ◇ What sins do you need to confess and repent? Take time and do it.
- ◇ Ask the Holy Spirit to fill you, and commit to walk with him.

SECTION 7

"WHO STRENGTHENS ME"

God gives us the strength we need to pursue our God-given dreams and goals and help us reach our full potential in Christ.

"I can do all things through Christ **who strengthens me**."

CHAPTER 19
ZIKLAG

We will receive strength from God to accomplish what he has called us to do.

"Whoever serves, let him serve as one who serves by the strength that God supplies."

1 PETER 4:11

"Be sure of this, when you least expect it the Lord will break through with help, perfectly timed, magnificently suited to your needs."

LLOYD JOHN OGILVIE, *THE ESSENCE OF HIS PRESENCE*

Strength: The capacity of an object to exert great power and withstand great pressure.

Every morning, Bob Moore wakes up to a bowl of oatmeal. He is still going strong in his nineties and does not plan to stop! He is the founder of Bob's Red Mill, a whole grains food company that sells products in over eighty countries with revenue of over one hundred million dollars.

Bob's journey into whole grains began with the convergence

of three life forces: whole grains, gristmills, and God. In the 1960s, Bob's wife, Charlee (now deceased), received books from her grandmother on eating healthy whole grains. Charlee began to incorporate whole grains into the family diet—a rarity in the days of white bread and TV dinners. The couple came to believe that healthy eating and whole grains were a gift from God.

The second life-force convergence was when Bob picked up and read a copy of George Woodbury's book, *John Goffe's Mill*. It is the story of an archeologist who inherits and restores a gristmill. Bob thought, *If he can do it, so can I*. Moore found stone mills for grinding wheat, had them shipped to California from North Carolina, and started Moore's Flour Mill in Redding, California.

The third convergence came in 1978. Bob and Charlee sold the mill to their son and moved to Oregon so Bob could attend seminary and study the Bible in the original languages. While walking around the community and memorizing Greek words written on flashcards, Bob saw an old mill for sale and bought it. The Moores could not seem to get away from the whole grains business. They worked hard, and the mill did well. Bob and Charlee were set to turn a hefty profit in 1988 until an arsonist set fire to the mill and burned it to the ground. The only things that survived were the stone mill grinders.

Emotionally devastated and financially decimated, Bob and Charlee had to discern what God wanted them to do. They prayed and decided the world needed healthy whole grain and gluten-free food. They took out a loan and rebuilt the mill! Their dependence on God and perseverance paid dividends.

Through the years of building a business, when discouragement and setbacks would have made anyone want to quit, Bob and Charlee were bolstered by the strength of God and love for what they were called to do. They built their business on the Golden Rule: "Do unto others as you would have them do to you." They believed in making a great product and treating their employees and customers right.[98] God gave them success.

We are as strong as the power of Christ in us! Let me encourage you: God *will* give strength to accomplish all he has set out for us to do—no matter how long it takes or how hard it seems. As Paul said the Philippians, "For I am confident in this, that He who began a good work in you will be faithful to complete it until the day of Christ Jesus" (Philippians 1:6).

He went on to say, "God is working in you both to will and to work for his good pleasure" (Philippians 2:13); God does this through the power of the Holy Spirit within us and God orchestrating the circumstances around us in order to accomplish the plans he has for us.

RECAP

Let's review Philippians 4:13 and the connected theme:

- ◊ "I": We have taken responsibility for our lives.
- ◊ "CAN": We believe we can reach our God-given dreams.
- ◊ "DO": We are taking action steps to achieve our goals.
- ◊ "ALL THINGS": We have clarity and purpose in what we believe God wants us to do.
- ◊ "THROUGH CHRIST": We realize Christ is working through us by the power of the Holy Spirit.

This final section of the book is about the power of God to strengthen us. We have a plan, but where do we get the power

---

98 https://www.bobsredmill.com/bobs-way/meet-bob-and-charlee-moore

to perform? What do we depend on when our plans hit the wall? Where do we go when we want to quit? What do we do when we don't know what to do? What resources avail themselves when we are mentally, physically, and spiritually exhausted?

When we think about these questions, we realize we need power greater than our own.

SOME ARE STRONGER THAN OTHERS

Some individuals are naturally stronger than others. For instance, my brother is 6'4"; I am not—two men from the same parents, yet physically very different.

Some people are gifted with talent beyond the norm. Some are born with more empathy; they have naturally stronger caring skills. Like it or not, some are born with innate strength or a knack for a certain area. The good news is that we too can become strong in things that do not come naturally; we just have to work harder and longer.

Some People Are Physically Stronger than Others

In gym class, the teacher sometimes picked me and another boy to be opposing team leaders, and the two of us would take turns picking the other kids until everyone in the class was on a team. I always picked the strongest and the fastest first because I knew it would give us a better chance of winning. My friends did not always like it because I did not choose them immediately, but I wanted to win. I wasn't that big, so even before understanding the principle as a rule of management, I instinctively "hired to my weakness."

Some People Are Mentally Stronger than Others

Some people are born with a higher degree of mental toughness. They have a greater capacity to endure hardship and stress. I once read about an Army officer who could go for days without loss of focus while averaging about two hours of sleep a night. I am amazed by the tenacity of some soldiers who spent years in POW camps, suffering daily abuse and deprivation yet never breaking. Part of their strength comes from training, but some of it is because of the way they are mentally wired.

Some People Are Intellectually Stronger than Others

The Mensa society was created to gather a community of people with an IQ in the top 2 percent of the population. They have a greater intellectual capacity. Some people are naturally smarter than others.

Some People Are Socially Stronger than Others

Some people are born with a "type A" personality that gives them a natural drive to get things done. Some are born extroverts who naturally connect with people and can inject themselves into any social situation with comfort and ease. Some are natural connectors with a high likeability factor.

Having natural strength, gifts, and talents does not make any person better than another. We are all made in the image of God, and we each have value and worth. God is sovereign in how he has wired us, and, again, we should not "think more highly of ourselves than we ought" (Romans 12:3). Instead, we should be thankful to God for how he has made us and develop our strengths for his glory and service. We can also grow in the areas of need.

Were you were born with greater natural strength in certain areas? Super! We rejoice with you! But always remember, accomplishing God-given goals and dreams will require God's strength. We cannot do it on our own or under our own power.

We will all go through times when we need more strength than we can naturally muster. In fact, reaching our full potential in Christ cannot be done without his power. Jesus said, "For apart from me you can do nothing" (John 15:5).

WHEN DO WE NEED GOD'S STRENGTH?

Knowing a formula for success does not insulate us against the difficulty we can encounter in reaching our goals. There may be times of discomfort, doubt, loss of direction, delay, discouragement, disfunction, despair, and lack of desire. Success is hard, and man-made formulas, as good as they may be, are not enough to accomplish a God-sized task. We need his strength to endure.

When do we need his strength? I can think of the following instances, and you may add your own:

- ◇ When I want to shirk my responsibility. Taking personal responsibility for my success is necessary. The problem is I sometimes want to give it back. I'm like a child who wants to give up their puppy when they realize they have to keep on feeding and cleaning up after it.

- ◇ When my faith grows weak and I'm tempted to doubt.

- ◇ When I am physically tired of taking action and grow weary in the work.

- ◇ When I want to procrastinate instead of remaining focused.

- ◇ When adversity and setbacks seem to come in waves.

- ◇ When I want to give up and quit.

- When I reach a plateau.
- When it seems too hard.
- When I run out of resources.
- When I face opposition.
- When I am being criticized.
- When I feel defeated.
- When I have messed up.
- When my sin seems to get the best of me.
- When my dreams/goals are delayed.
- When I realize that God is sending me in a different direction. Remember that the apostle Paul wanted to go to Asia to preach the gospel, but God spoke to him by a dream and redirected him to Macedonia. We need God's strength when we realize it is time to pivot in a new direction.

As we look to Scripture, we can find many examples of men and women who faced seemingly insurmountable tasks yet depended on the strength of God to see them through. Let's look at few.

KING DAVID HAD THE STRENGTH OF GOD

King David was a man after God's own heart (1 Samuel 13:14, Acts 13:22). As a young man, he was anointed king of Israel by Samuel, the high priest, though it would be many years before David ascended to the throne. David is described as a "man of valor, a man of war, prudent in matters and good looking, and the Lord is with him" (1 Samuel 16:18). He killed the giant, Goliath, and was given one of the daughters of King Saul as a wife. His popularity increased with the people. So did the jealousy of King Saul toward his young son-in-law.

David was forced to flee Jerusalem, and remained on the run from Saul for perhaps as long as a decade. The future king had to live in caves and forests to avoid capture and certain death. Fatigued by Saul's pursuits, David decided to escape to the land of the Philistines where he made an alliance with Achish, the king of Gath. David and his army, which had grown to six hundred men, settled in Ziklag for over a year.

While based in Ziklag, David maintained peace with the Philistines. He and his army also conducted raids against the Geshurites, the Girzites, and the Amalekites—Israel's ancient enemies. Once, while David and his army were three days away in Jezreel, the Amalekites invaded David's home base of Ziklag. They burned the town and kidnapped the women and children and carried them away. David and his army returned to the empty ruins of their fortress. Shocked by the devastation, they wept and wailed aloud until they had no more strength (1 Samuel 30:4). So grieved was the army over the loss of their families that the soldiers became bitter at David and spoke of stoning him.

What was David to do? He must have been at the end of his rope. He had been traveling for three days with little to no rest. He was an exile from Israel and an enemy of Saul. He had just learned that all of his possessions were gone and his family was kidnapped. To add insult to injury, his own army blamed him for their predicament and wanted to kill him!

David had no strength of his own, but he was not without strength. He was laid low but still had life and the will to come back. Instead of accepting defeat, David "strengthened himself in the Lord" and asked God what he should do (1 Samuel 30:6–8). God told him to pursue the Amalekites. David gathered his army, struck down the Amalekites, rescued his family, and retrieved all of the stolen goods!

What do we do when we get tired, feel alone, suffer loss, don't know what to do, and want to quit? What do we do when we are depleted of our own power? We do as David did. He sought the help of God, and God gave David *his* strength.

HABAKKUK HAD THE STRENGTH OF GOD

The prophet Habakkuk lived in trying times. The nation of Judah was in spiritual and moral decay. God gave a dire message to the perplexed prophet, one the people of Judah would not believe: God was going to use the eviler nation of Babylon to punish the less evil nation of Judah. The prophecy was fulfilled in 586 BC when Nebuchadnezzar II laid siege to Jerusalem, destroying the temple and carrying many Israelites to exile.

Habakkuk's prophetic ministry may have gone on for over thirty years. Can you imagine the emotional and spiritual turmoil of preaching judgment for that long while seeing little to no evidence that the people were having a change of heart? Habakkuk prayed, poured out his complaints to God, prophesied to the people, and continued progressing in the work God called him to do.

How did he do it? How was he able to push on in the midst of rejection and disappointment? Where did he generate the strength he needed to go on when he became weary? Did he have greater natural ability to endure pain? No. Habakkuk had a supernatural strength that came from God. He says so in the last verses of his book: "Though the fig tree shall not blossom, and there be no fruit on the vines; though the olive tree fails to bear fruit and the fields produce no crop; the flock shall be cut off from the fold, and no cattle be in the stalls: Yet I will take joy in the God of my salvation. *The Lord is my strength*, and he will make my feet like a deer, and make me to walk on the mountain" (Habakkuk 3:17–19; emphasis added).

Habakkuk's name means "to embrace" or "to cling to." He held on to God and endured the onslaught of opposition he faced from hostile forces. A strong God is the believer's strength.

PAUL THE APOSTLE HAD THE STRENGTH OF GOD

We tend to think of Paul as something of a Christian superhero—traveling the Roman world, preaching the gospel, and starting churches. Paul stood up to religious bullies and haters. He wrote most of the New Testament letters, sometimes while imprisoned. He spoke truth to power without wavering to their trappings. He was the most decorated combatant of spiritual warfare. He was truly an amazing man.

Paul was also a super-survivor. He endured much pain and hardship in his service to Christ. He was beaten with forty lashes by the Jews on five different occasions. Three times he was beaten with rods. Once he was stoned and left for dead. He was shipwrecked three times and often in danger from muggers, robbers, Jews, and Gentiles. He endured toil, hardship, sleepless nights, hunger and thirst, cold, and deprivation. In addition to physical maladies and difficulties, he maintained constant care and concern for the churches under his charge. He recounts his personal "survivor list" in 2 Corinthians 11:16–30.

The apostle Paul could "take a whoopin and keep on cookin" because his strength came from God, and he constantly expressed his gratitude: "I thank Christ Jesus our Lord, who has strengthened me, because He considered me faithful, putting me into service" (1 Timothy 1:12 NASB).

GOD WILL GIVE US STRENGTH!

God will give us strength as well. Sometimes we get to the point of thinking, *This is all I can do*. With the strength of God, our thought should be *Who knows what all I can do!* Lean on God for strength. Lean into what he has called you to do.

When you think you have done all you can do, tap into what God can do through you. God the Father, Son, and Holy Spirit will empower us with strength beyond human imagination.

God the Father Will Give Us Strength

Psalms 46:1 says, "God is our refuge and strength, a very present help in time of trouble."

The Almighty God who created the universe is present within us. The sovereign king of history has a place for us in his story. He loves us just as much as any person portrayed in the Bible. He gives us strength to soar like a majestic eagle. He is our source of strength, especially in time of need.

God the Son Will Give Us Strength

The epistle to the Hebrews states, "For consider Him who has endured such hostility by sinners against Himself, so that you will not grow weary and lose heart" (Hebrews 12:3).

Jesus died so we may live. His strength is made perfect in our weakness. The power of his cross is greater than our desire to quit. His passion is reason to press on. His work at Calvary is strength to overcome weakness. Jesus said, "Very truly, I say to you, he who believes in me, the works that I do, he shall do also; and greater works than these he will do; because I go to the Father" (John 14:12). Not only will Jesus give us strength, but he will also give us "greater works" strength!

Paul Anderson is considered to be one of the strongest men to ever live. He was born in Toccoa, Georgia, on October 17, 1932. As a child, he struggled with Bright's disease, a kidney ailment that would contribute to his death at age sixty-one. In his prime, he stood five feet nine inches and weighed 375 pounds with thighs thirty-six inches around. The Russians nicknamed him "Chudo Piryody," which means "wonder of nature." Designations from other admirers included "strongest man alive" and "Gospel Giant of Georgia."

During his career as a weight lifter, Anderson set four official Olympic weight-lifting records (clean and press, snatch, clean and jerk, and total weight). He was listed in the 1985 Guinness Book of World Records as well as Famous First Facts for his 6,270-pound back lift, the greatest weight ever lifted by a human being. Over a four-year span, Paul became a world champion, Olympic champion, two-time US national champion, and set eighteen American records and eight world records.

Anderson also enjoyed displaying more unusual feats of strength. He could drive a twenty-penny nail through a two-inch board with his fist. He could lift two 85-pound dumbbells with his little fingers, and pick up a table with eight men sitting on it.

Paul went to the 1956 Olympics in Melbourne, Australia, with a severe inner-ear infection and a 103-degree fever. Having fallen far behind the front-runners in the competition, his only chance for the gold medal was to set a new Olympic record in the clean and jerk at 413.5 pounds. His first two attempts missed the mark. He had one try left. Before his third and final attempt, Paul prayed to God for extra help and strength. God answered his prayer, and Paul won the gold! Later he would say, "I wasn't making a bargain. I needed help."

Along with his wife, Glenda, Paul opened the Paul Anderson Youth Home in Vidalia, Georgia in 1961. The objective was to "strive to provide a Christ-centered, holistic, and therapeutic approach toward transforming the lives of young men between the ages of 16-21." The home has been in operation for over fifty years.

In order to provide funding for the home, Paul would make over five hundred appearances a year and include his testimony to the saving and sustaining power of Jesus Christ. Anderson always included a challenge to his audience: "If the strongest man in the world can't get through one day without the power of Jesus Christ, where does that leave you?"[99]

God the Holy Spirit Will Give Us Strength

To the Ephesians Paul wrote, "I pray that God would grant you, according to the riches of his glory, to be strengthened with power through his Spirit in the inner man" (Ephesians 3:16).

The Holy Spirit will hang in when we are ready to quit and check out. He will strengthen us beyond human measure. He will teach us what we cannot learn, protect us when we are vulnerable, guide us when we don't know where to go, renew our drive when we are out of spiritual gas, and make us willing by his filling!

CONCLUSION

Life's circumstances can be overwhelming. Even when we are doing what we believe God has called us to do, we face obstacles and difficulties. The good news is that God supplies when we are depleted. As Pastor Erwin Lutzer said, "A faithful God does not expect you to do what you cannot; He supplies the needed strength."[100] The omnipotent God of the universe supplies power to us.

---

99 October 13, 2015, https://christianindex.org/20151015-weight-lifter-paul-anderson/, Ron F. Hale

100 https://www.allchristianquotes.org/index.php?v=page&c=topics&s=6670&l=Tell

CAN DO; GO DO

- ◇ Refer back to the Scripture verses used in this chapter on God's strength. Can you think of others?
- ◇ Ask God for "greater works" strength and go after what you are too weak to do on your own.

CHAPTER 20
REBAR

God is the source and force of strength. He also provides resources to help us grow in his strength.

"Blessed is the man whose strength is in You.... They go from strength to strength; Each one appears before God in Zion."

PSALMS 84:5,7

Growing stronger in Christ weakens the power of sin.

We all need the strength of God, and he graciously gives us the help we need. I can remember times as a pastor when, at the end of the day, there was much left to do: sermons to prepare, people to counsel, and meetings to attend. Yet I was at the end of my ability. I wanted to go home and call it a day, but the needs of the job could not be postponed. I felt like the psalmist when he said, "In my distress I called upon the Lord; to my God I cried for help. From his temple he heard my voice, and my cry to him reached his ears" (Psalms 18:6). Thankfully, God came through as needed, and I could get done what was needed. We should never forget that God is holding on to us when we are at the end of our rope.

Concrete is a mixture of cement, sand, gravel, and water. It is used for sidewalks and building foundations because it has great compression strength. It is tough to bust. When concrete is reinforced with steel rebar, it becomes exponentially stronger and can be used to build bridges and skyscrapers. Steel rebar increases the tensile strength of the concrete. With greater tensile strength, concrete resists cracking and breaking under tension.

God's strength is like rebar giving exponential strength to our life. He keeps us from cracking and breaking under the tension of the detrimental forces that deplete our power. With the rebar strength of God, we can build a life that goes higher and spans farther than we ever imagined. Like a construction worker mixing concrete, God expects us to mix in certain additives that increase the strength of our being. The following is not a complete list but are, I believe, essential components of growing in the strength God provides.

BEING HUMBLE AND ADMITTING WE ARE WEAK

Even the apostle Paul had his limitations. He called his condition a "thorn in the flesh, a messenger of Satan to torment me" (2 Corinthians 12:7). Yet he declared, "Therefore, for Christ's sake, I will delight in weaknesses . . . for when I am weak, then I am strong" (2 Corinthians 12:10). Scripture does not give us much detail on the nature of the "thorn." It may have been spiritual, physical, relational, emotional, or any other category of Paul's life wheel. We don't know his exact ailment, but we do know it was a constant struggle—so much so that he asked God to remove it from him. God did not take it away but instead gave him grace to live with it.

Perhaps we are left ignorant of the nature of Paul's thorn so that we can identify with the predicament. We all have some kind of thorn, something that nags at us, irritates us, and is a constant source of struggle. My thorn may not be your thorn, but we all have situations that we feel powerless to overcome.

Having the Holy Spirit certainly helps, but he does not make us superhuman. We are limited in our personal power. We need to be humble enough to admit we need the strength of God. Then we will understand that weakness is a grace gift from God to cause us to depend on him and operate in his strength.

GROWING "INNER MAN" STRENGTH FROM SCRIPTURE AND PRAYER

Psalms 1:1–3 explains, "*Blessed* is the man [or woman] that walks not in the counsel of the ungodly, nor stands in the way of sinners, nor sits in the seat of the scornful, but his *delight* is in the *law of the Lord,* and in his law he does *meditate* both day and night. He shall be like a tree, planted by the rivers of water, that brings forth its fruit in its season, whose leaf also shall not wither; and *whatsoever he does shall prosper*" (emphasis added).

We believe God wants us to succeed in our endeavors. He wants us to "prosper" in life's pursuits. It is a given that God is for us as we seek to succeed and reach our God-given potential in Christ.

In the process of success, we will encounter spiritual warfare. The world, the flesh, and the devil will fight against us. For example, some people will discourage us instead of encouraging us. There may be times when someone sticks out a foot to trip us instead of lending a hand to help. The world will tell us that we can't do it. Our flesh will go through periods of weakness, discouragement, sin, and setbacks. The devil will seek to steal, kill, and destroy our God-given dreams. How do we cross the finish line? We grow our "inner man [or woman]" strength.

Inner man strength is the spiritual and mental toughness the believer develops. Inner man strength requires inner man resources. Our personal willpower is not strong enough to accomplish God's work. We have to develop a relationship with God. Knowing God is more important than accomplishing any dream. In fact, knowing God is the ultimate dream! The apostle Paul proudly declared that all of his accomplishments were nothing compared to the surpassing worth of knowing Christ (Philippians 3:8).

The way to know Christ is by devoting ourselves to him through Scripture and prayer. I have mentioned these two vital resources before, and it stands repeating. Willpower is made stronger by Word power! It is essential to have a regular time with God where we study the Bible and pray for God to give us understanding, faith, and a heart to obey. Charles Spurgeon agreed when he said, "We should be better Christians if we were more alone, waiting upon God, and gathering through meditation on His Word spiritual strength for labour in His service."[101]

Prayer

God does not need to be *reminded* of the dreams he has placed in our hearts. We need to *remember* that he is the one that gave them to us. Prayer reminds us of our need for God's strength in the pursuit of the dreams and goals he has given us. As Paul wrote to the Philippians, "Be anxious for nothing, but in everything by prayer and supplication with thanksgiving, let your requests be made known unto God. And the peace of God, which passes all understanding, will guard your heart and mind by Christ Jesus" (Philippians 4:6–7).

---

[101] https://www.spurgeon.org/resource-library/sermons/quiet-musing/#flipbook/

Bible

The author of Psalms pleads, "My soul is weary with sorrow; strengthen me according to your word" (Psalms 119:28).

God's Word reaches through the mind and heart and strengthens us at the very core of our being. When we are physically, emotionally, and spiritually depleted, God will use his words to strengthen us.

Two benefits of the habit of Scripture and prayer come readily to mind: One, it *fortifies* us against the ungodly, sinners, and scornful people who would tell us we are not good enough, or that God is not with us, or that our dreams are unattainable. Secondly, it energizes our *faith* to persevere when we are tempted to doubt God's power working through us.

STAYING HOPEFUL

To have hope is to be confident that God will deliver us and deliver for us—in his own time and in his own way. It is a close relative of faith but different, partially in timing. For instance, faith is more of a virtue that spurs us to immediate action. Hope keeps us going for the long haul. Faith in Christ is what saves us. Hope in his promise of eternal life in heaven sustains us and empowers us to keep going. Hope has an expectation of a good outcome. Faith trusts God no matter the outcome. What does hope look like? The following HOPE acronym can give us a picture.

Help from God

Psalms 121:1–2 declares, "I will lift my eyes to the hills. From where does my help come from? My help comes from the Lord, the maker of heaven and earth."

Hope grows stronger when we seek God's help. Why? Because in seeking the help of God, we realize we need power that is greater than our own. We also remember that he desires to help us! Every great character in the Bible shares the common trait of seriously seeking help from God.

Many times, God will send help through other people. Don't be afraid to ask for help. Find people who are where you want to be, and ask them to help you get there. Successful people want to share their secrets. If you are stuck, ask someone who has gone through the same experience and gotten "unstuck." Do you need to hire a coach, see a counselor, phone a friend, or talk to your pastor? Take action! Get help, and God will reinforce your strength.

Optimistic Outlook

A good attitude will take us a lot further than a bad one. Developing a positive attitude is essential for staying hopeful and being hope-filled. According to author Brendon Burchard, "Positive emotion, in general, is one of the greatest predictors of the good life—high energy and high performance. . . . Neuroscientists have even found that positive emotions prompt new cell growth (plasticity), whereas negative emotions cause decay."[102] Hope grows our hearts and our heads!

Many people are born with a bent toward the negative, focusing more on what could go wrong than what will go right. We downplay our strengths and heighten our weaknesses. It is part of our sin nature. This is one reason why stress, anxiety, and depression are so prevalent in our world. People have lost hope. While it is a good idea to consider what could go wrong and mitigate on the front end, we should pursue our goals with an optimistic attitude that we will reach them and have a successful outcome.

---

102 Brendon Burchard, *High Performance Habits* (New York: Hay House, 2017), 104.

Hope grows by choosing to believe in the greatness of God—that he is with us and working all things for our good. Because of him, we have reason to be optimistic about life! As Paul wrote to the Romans, "Now may the God of hope fill you with all joy and peace in believing, so that you may overflow with hope by the power of the Holy Spirit" (Romans 15:13).

Passionate Purpose

Paul wrote the Corinthians, "For in this hope [our redemption through the resurrection and return of Jesus] we are saved. . . . For if we hope for what we do not see, we wait for it with patience" (1 Corinthians 15:10).

Our purpose is our reason for living. It is why we get up in the morning and keep going throughout the day. Purpose is what turns tinkerers into inventors and hobbyists into skilled pros. It turns a job into a calling and gives direction to those who have detoured from their life map.

Every Christian has been given the dual passionate purpose of living by the Great Commandment and seeking to fulfill the Great Commission: "You shall love the Lord your God with all of your heart, and with all your soul, and with all your mind, and with all your strength. The second is this, you shall love your neighbor as yourself" (Mark 12:30–31 NASB). The Great Commission is the mandate Jesus gave to all of his followers to spread the gospel and make disciples: "Go into all the world and make disciples of all nations, baptizing them in the name of the Father and the Son and the Holy Spirit, teaching them to obey all I have commanded you" (Matthew 28:19–20). Whatever goal, job, career, or endeavor we undertake should be subservient to this overriding principle that our purpose is to love God and people and make disciples for Christ.

In addition to the scriptural purposes just mentioned, God also gives us individual dreams and purposes. David Green combined his love for God with a passion for retail sales to create Hobby Lobby. He said, "Retail was such a joyous contrast to the rest of my life. . . . I had finally found something I was good at." In 1970, David and his wife, Barbara, took out a six-hundred-dollar loan and started making picture frames on their kitchen table. David continued to work a full-time job at a retail store. In 1972, he opened his first store. Today there are nine hundred Hobby Lobby stores with forty-three thousand employees.

Hobby Lobby is committed to great customer service as well as respecting their employees. Part of the company's core values is "serving [their] employees and their families by establishing a work environment and company policies that build character, strengthen individuals and nurture families."[103]

The Green family is also committed to philanthropy. The company gives 50 percent of pretax profits to Christian organizations that minister all over the world, including schools, evangelistic ministries, and benevolence concerns. The Green family also founded the Museum of the Bible in Washington, DC. Green said, "We believe it is by God's grace and provision that Hobby Lobby has endured. He has been faithful in the past, we trust Him for our future."[104]

Find your purpose in God, and live your passion. Consider the following story.

Three bricklayers are working on a wall when a curious passerby asks the first one, "What are you doing?"

"I am laying bricks" is the reply.

The second bricklayer responds, "I'm building a church wall to feed my family."

The third bricklayer, with a smile on his face and humming a hymn, replies, "I'm building a cathedral for God where people can worship him!"

---

[103] https://newsroom.hobbylobby.com/corporate-background/
[104] Taken from David Green, *More than a Hobby*, (Nashville, Thomas Nelson, 2005)

The first bricklayer had something to do. The second had a job that met his needs. The third bricklayer had a passionate purpose.

Enduring Expectation

Paul said, "Let us run with endurance the race that is set before us, looking to Jesus" (Hebrews 12:1–2).

A person with hope is in it for the long haul. They are a go-getter, not a quick quitter. Someone with hope can push through the hard times because they expect to win the prize. Hope has an enduring quality that gives energy in the pursuit and a confident expectation that God will help us achieve our goals.

Life can seem more like hoisting the rock of Sisyphus than resting in the Rock of Ages (a.k.a. Jesus Christ). Hope keeps us from despair. Early believers were characterized by hope. They had the enduring expectation that the sufferings, trials, persecutions, and hardships of this earthly life would eventually give way to the bliss of eternal life in heaven with Jesus. They believed the words of Jesus when he said, "Because I live, you shall live also" (John 14:19).

Hope is assurance that even though we have not achieved, we work as if we have and until we do. Abraham lived with expectancy that he would father a child. After it was long past his and Sarah's natural ability to conceive, God delivered, and Isaac was born. Abraham was fully convinced that God would do as he had promised, and he endured until the promise was fulfilled (Romans 4:21). That is enduring expectation. The strength to do all things comes through the power of Christ in us. Having hope helps! As Paul explained to the Roman church, "Now hope does not disappoint, because the love of God has been poured into our hearts through the Holy Spirit who has been given to us" (Romans 5:5).

Endurance, perseverance, resilience—call it what you will,

but the outcome is the same. We have to keep going until we reach our goals. Hope turns the potential stumbling blocks of setback, adversity, pain, and disappointment into stepping stones on a victorious walk. As the old Japanese proverb says, "Fall down seven times, get up eight."

In 1980, Terry Fox entered the Marathon of Hope to raise money for cancer research. He was a hardworking athlete who had lost a leg to cancer in 1977. Terry's goal was to run all the way across Canada. He ran the equivalent of a marathon a day for 143 days, covering the equivalent of 3,339 miles before having to cut short the excursion due to a recurrence of cancer in his lungs. Terry died a few months later, shortly before his twenty-third birthday.

Terry had to endure much hardship during his run. On the first day, he ran in gale-force winds, rain, and a snowstorm. Over the weeks of running, he had personal conflicts with his van driver. Terry also fought the physical pain of running on an artificial leg. When asked how he kept going when he was exhausted and there were so many miles ahead, he replied, "I just keep running to the next telephone pole."[105]

The annual Terry Fox run for cancer research has raised hundreds of millions of dollars to fight the disease. Speaking at a fundraiser before his death, Terry said, "Everybody seems to have given up hope of trying. I haven't. It isn't easy and it isn't supposed to be, but I'm accomplishing something."[106]

Hope makes things happen. Wishing wants something to happen but fails to take action. Wanting our ship to come in while not setting the sails is wishing. Hope weighs anchor, sets the sails to catch the wind, and sets a course to reach one's destiny. Stay hopeful!

---

[105] Jack Canfield, *The Success Principles* (New York: Harper Collins, 2005), 173.
[106] https://canadaehx.com/2020/06/28/the-marathon-of-hope/

GETTING HEALTHY

I love pastors and the work they do. I served as one for twenty-two years. Most pastors have an active mind and a relatively sedentary lifestyle. At times, the most exercise I got was walking from the pew to the pulpit on Sunday. The hours of ministry by meetings can be long, and mental exhaustion discourages physical exercise. Pray for your pastor's health.

Every year, we pastors would go to the annual convention of our denomination, and I noticed that a number of us were overweight. Our denomination could see it as well. They offered a free health assessment to any pastor at the convention. As I remember, the waiting line was not long at that booth. Maybe we did not want to stand that long. Seems the healthiest part of our bodies was our appetite.

Pastors are not alone. Seems we are, to a *large* degree, a reflection of the congregations we serve. In the United States, 60 percent of the population is overweight or obese. This does not merely result from lack of exercise. Americans also eat too much. Such poor lifestyle choices lead to lack of energy, increased risk of depression, and many other health risks, such as heart disease, cancer, and diabetes. The annual estimated health-care costs of obesity-related illness is approaching two hundred billion.[107]

Our bodies are temples of the Holy Spirit. God expects us to take care of them. It seems somewhat hypocritical to neglect our health and pray for strength (though I admit I do, and, thankfully, God has mercy). Studies suggest that proper nutrition (diet), exercise, and proper sleep may increase serotonin levels in the brain and boost feelings of hope. Being healthier will naturally

---

107 https://www.healthycommunitieshealthyfuture.org/learn-the-facts/economic-costs-of-obesity/

increase our strength and make us feel better as well. Our health is our wealth! Good health helps makes us stronger.

LIVING HOLY

Paul explained to Timothy, "There is benefit to bodily exercise, but godliness benefits in every way, having promise for the present life as well as the life to come" (1 Timothy 4:8).

To live holy means our attitudes and actions are in line with what pleases God. We belong to him and place him at the center of our lives. This form of living includes seeking to live a moral life as a result of being in a saving relationship with Christ. As the reverend Dr. Joel Scandrett said, "To be holy means that all we have belongs to God, not ourselves, and every aspect of our lives is shaped and directed toward God."[108] Does living holy mean we will never sin? No. Jesus alone meets that standard. It means that when we sin, we will quickly turn from it, confess it to God, and ask forgiveness.

Obedience to God from the heart is the key to holiness. As Jesus said, "If you keep my commandments, you will abide in my love. . . . You are my friends if you do what I command you" (John 15:10,14). Living in the power of God requires obedience. Holy living means we have a desire to live right by God through following the Scripture. It is heartfelt because we are convinced it is God's way of living and the best way for us to live: "For this is the love of God, that we keep his commandments, and his commandments are not burdensome" (1 John 5:3).

Living in obedience to God, by the power of God, strengthens our desire to please God.

---

108 https://www.christianitytoday.com/biblestudies/bible-answers/theology/what-does-god-mean-when-he-asks-us-to-be-holy.html?start=2

HELPING OTHERS

Paul asked the Galatians, "For you have been called to freedom, my brethren, only do not use your freedom to satisfy the flesh, but through love serve one another" (Galatians 5:13).

Serving is a synonym for helping. Striving to reach our goals and dreams can become self-centered as well as self-serving. If we are not careful, we will begin to look at people only in relation to how they can help us achieve our dreams. Such an attitude is contrary to the purpose of achieving our God-given goals, which includes glorifying God and doing good to others. Helping others is like a bonding agent that strengthens relationships and makes us stronger.

There was an elderly lady in our church who needed some yard work. She said she would pay to have her yard mowed and cleaned. I volunteered my young teenage son. It was summer, and I figured he needed something to do besides playing video games. The lady did not have a lawnmower, so we put ours and a weed eater in the back of the Suburban and headed to her house. When we got there, she definitely needed yard work, both front and back. I don't think it had seen any TLC for many moons. It was so bad that I did not think it fair to make my son do it all by himself, so I stayed and helped.

We mowed grass, trimmed around trees, raked up brush, and drank a lot of water. It took hours, but the yard looked nice from all sides. The lady was overjoyed by how good it looked. My son rightly expected a big payday but was naturally disappointed when she paid him all of seven dollars. I was disappointed for him. But at the same time, he learned a lesson that ministry is serving people who do not, or cannot, always help in return. He never complained, but when asked if he could do it the next week, he gave her the names of two other boys who lived closer to her. His daddy didn't raise no dummy!

PLAYING HURT

During the journeys of Paul and Barnabas, they returned to Antioch to motivate their followers there, "strengthening the souls of the disciples, encouraging them to continue in the faith, and saying that through many tribulations we must enter the kingdom of God" (Acts 14:22).

William Green was a first-round pick for the Cleveland Browns in the 2002 NFL draft. In his rookie season, he rushed for almost nine hundred yards and helped the Browns reach the playoffs for the first time in eight years.

William's life was not without pain and problems. He grew up in a tough New Jersey neighborhood. Both his parents died while he was a teenager, and he was separated from his brothers and sister.

William was great at football in high school and college and made it into the NFL. He had a promising career in the pros, but some of his off-the-field issues likely contributed to its brevity. Injuries, poor choices, and lack of focus took a toll on the star running back. The good news is Green's life turned around when he came to faith in Christ.

After retiring from football, Green remembered many valuable life lessons he learned from his experiences, coaches, and mentors. One is about making good choices. He said, "You are not born a winner or a loser but a chooser." Another one is about perseverance and the desire to improve: "It's not how you start but how you finish."

A final thematic quote from Green that resonates with

audiences is about working through the hurts of life. Michael recounted how in football, toward the end of the season, everyone experienced the bodily hurts of four or more months of a full-contact football season. He told me, "Everyone plays through the hurt; the key is not to play injured."

Playing through the hurt is part of life as well as football. By the grace of God, we can grow stronger through the hurt. "No pain, no gain," as many athletes would say. We all face the hurts of disappointments, defeat, and difficulty. Sometimes they come as a result of our own doing. Sometimes they are part of God's re-doing us into the image of Christ: "For the moment all discipline seems painful rather than pleasant, but later it yields the peaceful fruit of righteousness to those who have been trained by it" (Hebrews 12:11).

Just remember, if you get injured, make time to heal.

BEING HAPPY

Nehemiah told the people of Jerusalem, "The joy of the Lord is your strength" (Nehemiah 8:10).

Nehemiah was used by God at a critical time for the nation of Israel to lead the people to rebuild the wall around Jerusalem and renew their devotion to God. The wall was miraculously completed in fifty-two days, against much opposition. Shortly after completion, Nehemiah called the Israelites to renew their covenant to God and celebrate the Feast of Booths.

During the celebration, the people gathered together to hear the reading of the book of the Law. While listening, they began to weep and mourn because they realized they had been disobedient to God and had not been faithful in following the Word of God. They were sorry for sinning in such a manner.

Instead of exhorting them in their remorse, Nehemiah encouraged the people to celebrate by joyfully renewing their covenant devotion to the God of Israel. He inspired them to be internally joyful as God's chosen people.

The last time I checked, there were 751 million Google results for the "key to happiness." Answers include everything from having a certain level of income to going for a walk. Seems that everyone has an opinion on what it means to be happy, but few can actually define it or know it when they see it. Everyone likely wants to be happy, but few live in a state of happiness.

When most people think of happiness, they probably think of some external circumstance that causes an emotional response: like a child getting their favorite video game for Christmas, an adult getting a pay raise at work, or a sports team winning the championship. Such instances trigger positive emotions and short-term euphoria, but these generally don't last.

God is not opposed to the emotional state of being happy. Believers should certainly feel excitement in worship and the euphoria of encountering God. King David danced before the Lord when the Ark of the Covenant was brought to Jerusalem. Mary Magdalene and the other Mary experienced fear and great joy when the angel told them Jesus had risen from the dead (Matthew 28:8). There is nothing wrong with being happy in Jesus.

An emotional sense of happiness should also be the believer's response to answered prayer. God is very good to his people in allowing us to see the great things he does for us. Happiness and gratitude are appropriate responses to seeing the good hand of God in our lives and the world.

Joy and Contentment

Happy is not bad, and Scripture also refers to something deeper. It is called joy and contentment. These are more long lasting and internally generated. Joy and contentment signal satisfaction with God and life in good times as well as hard times. Happiness is an emotional, feeling experience when something good happens to us. Joy and contentment are enduring character traits the Holy Spirit instills in us. The apostle Paul learned this as he walked with Christ in every circumstance imaginable. He said, "For I have learned to be content in whatever situation I find myself" (Philippians 4:11).

My friend Len and I were on the last day of our mission trip in West Virginia to paint the ceiling tiles of a mobile home. We were about a fourth of the way finished when we realized that over half of our paint was gone. I called the organizer for more paint, but there was none. Nor could we get more at the store and come back the next day, because we were leaving early the following morning. We prayed God would stretch our paint, and he did! We were rubbing the inside of the paint can for that last drop. When we finished, the work looked beautiful, and the elderly couple who had not had their home painted probably ever could look up at a bright-white ceiling.

Earlier in the day, while talking and rolling paint on the walls, Len said to me, "Pastor Todd, I'm happy." I knew Len to be a man of strong faith and sincere love for God, so I was not surprised by his statement. What may be surprising to some is that Len could still say such a thing when he had been through some difficult circumstances, both inside and out of the church.

Len served in the Army in Vietnam and saw action in his tour of duty. Thankfully, God protected him against enemy fire. He made a career of the military and was promoted to the rank of first sergeant. After retiring, he and his wife, Jerrie, and their four daughters moved to the neighborhood not far from where I pastored.

Len and Jerrie eventually began attending the church and became members. They were very involved, with Jerrie working in children's ministry and Len serving as a deacon. We shared many wonderful experiences together and a few trying times when conflict arose in the congregation.

Len served with joy and took everything in stride. During one of the difficult days of ministry, I asked Len if he was having a good day. His response: "As long as no one is shooting at me, it's a good day." His words gave me perspective, and I realized that his source of joy and contentment was not the absence of conflict but the presence of Christ within him. The strength Len derived from the grace of God was the source and the force of his happiness.

The Attitude of Gratitude

One way to become happier is to show gratitude. Studies show that gratitude can improve general well-being, increase resilience, strengthen social relationships, and reduce stress and depression. Being grateful has the capacity to release the body's neurochemicals, such as dopamine and serotonin—natural body compounds known to contribute to feelings of happiness.[109]

Being thankful for what we have on the way to reaching our God-given goals and dreams will inspire us to keep going. Gratitude causes us to appreciate what we have rather than stress over what we want. As Charlotte Brontë put it, "Gratitude is a divine emotion: it fills the heart but not to bursting; it warms it but not to fever."[110]

---

109 https://www.heysigmund.com/the-science-of-gratitude/Karen Young
110 Charlotte Bronte, *Shirley* (New York: Penguin Classic ed., 2005).

CONCLUSION

Have you ever felt zapped of strength and physically, spiritually, or emotionally spent—perhaps all at the same time? Can you identify with a chewed-up piece of bubble gum spat out and walked over? Have you ever felt like your "Double Bubble" has become a wad of street glue imbedded in a worn, potholed road—sticky yet immovable, powerless and close to feeling lifeless?

Take heart! God can turn our gray, gummy goo into Juicy Fruit. With God there is hope, help, healing, and strength.

CAN DO; GO DO

- What are you struggling with that needs an infusion of God's strength?

- Look over the strength builders. What are one or two areas in which you can grow to become stronger? Pray for God to help.

EPILOGUE

The road to success is an uphill drive. There are switchbacks and detours, speed limits, stop signs, yield signs, and signs for falling rocks. Slow drivers, narrow passes, and stretches with no shoulder to turn on can hamper our progress. Accidents can bring traffic to a stop. Potholes can flatten a tire and damage the undercarriage. One has to watch out for speed traps and keep an eye on the fuel gauge.

But along the way are scenic views to give us perspective and exit ramps to refresh and refuel—and sometimes repair some broken parts. If we travel with friends, the journey becomes easier, and the ride to our destination seems quicker. With God as our guide, the journey will always be worthwhile. If we stay on the road, we will eventually arrive at our destination.

"I can do all things through Christ who strengthens me."

PHILIPPIANS 4:13

REFERENCES FROM NOTES

Chapter 2: Something Better than Self-Help

1 https://www.researchandmarkets.com/reports/4847127/the-us-market-for-self-improvement-products

2 https://www.jimrohn.com/self-improvement/

3 https://www.shortercatechism.com/resources/wsc/wsc001.html

Chapter 3: Blessed Burgers

4 Francis Chan, *Crazy Love: Overwhelmed by a Relentless God* (Colorado Springs, CO: David C. Cook, 2008), 93.

5 https://www.inspiringquotes.us/topic/6347-no-failure

6 https://moodycenter.org/the-quotable-moody-d-l-moody-quotes/

7 https://www.bereaninsights.org/quote/winston-churchill-quote

8 https://guidable.co/culture/5-common-japanese-proverbs-that-make-you-ponder

9 https://www.oprah.com/omagazine/what-oprah-knows-for-sure-about-finding-success

10 Earl Nightingale, *The Strangest Secret* (Merchant Books Online, 2013).

11 Joshua Metcalf and Jamie Gilbert, *Burn Your Goals*, (Morristown, NC: Lulu Publishing, 2015) 177.

12 http://www.skatewhat.com/russhowell/WebPage-Quotes-FloatingMenu.

13 https://laidlawscholars.network/posts/success-is-no-accident#:~:text=Pele

14 Charles Stanley, *Success God's Way* (Nashville: Thomas Nelson, 2000), 3.

15 https://billygraham.org/story/super-bowl-mvp-nick-foles-i-wouldnt-be-here-without-jesus-in- my-life/

16 https://www.epm.org/blog/2013/Jun/10/day-eternity

Chapter 4: God's Love Is Better Than Self-Love

17 https://www.mayoclinic.org/healthy-lifestyle/adult-health/in-depth/self-esteem/art-20047976

18 https://www.sciencedaily.com/release/2008/04/080428084235.htm

19 https://www.ncbi.nlm.nih.gov/pubmed/10626367

20 Rick Warren, *The Purpose Driven Life* (Grand Rapids, MI: Zondervan, 2002), 172.

Chapter 5: Fat-inization

21 https://www.livescience.com/13953-pigs-evolved-mud-wallowing.html

22 https://harveymackay.com/be-responsible-for-yourself/

Chapter 6: Dative Case

23 christiantoday.com.au/news/nick-vujicic-man-without-limbs-shares-the-bible-verse-that-gave-him-purpose.html

Chapter 7: Choose Your Hard

24 Brian Tracy, *No Excuses* (New York, NY: MJF Books, 2010), 50.

25 Dan Cathy, *The Problem in the Mirror*; Rightnow media.

26 Extreme Ownership | Jocko Willink | TEDxUniversityofNevada

27 Joelle Casteix, *The Power of Responsibility*, TedxPasadenaWomen

28 https://winstonchurchill.org/old-site/learn/speeches-learn/the-price-of-greatness/

Chapter 8: How to Become a Responsible Person

29 Adrian Rogers, *A Man of His Word*, DVD Curriculum Calling Men to Integrity and Leadership (Dallas, TX: Sampson Resources).

30 Alan Deutschman, *Change or Die* (New York: Harper, 2007), 14.

Chapter 9: Truing the Life Wheel

31 https://www.niddk.nih.gov/health-information/health-statistics/overweight-obesity

32 Rudyard Kipling, "If": https://poets.org/poem/if

33 https://guides.library.harvard.edu/c.php?g=880222&p=6323072

34 https://tremendousleadership.com/pages/Charlie

35 https://news.gallup.com/opinion/chairman/212045/world-broken-workplace

36 Dave Ramsey, *Dave Ramsey's Complete Guide to Money* (Brentwood, TN: Lampo Press, 2010).

37 https://www.resourceumc.org/en/content/john-wesley-on-giving

Chapter 10: Everyone Has It; Some Know It and Grow It

38 http://www.bpnews.net/48743/study-americans-fond-of-bible-but-how-many-read-it

39 https://www.youversion.com/the-bible-app/

40 https://www.crossway.org/articles/infographic-you-can-read-more-of-the-bible-than-you-think

42 https://utmost.org/classic/greater-works-classic/

43 https://www.georgemuller.org/quotes/category/trials/2

44 https://bibleportal.com/bible-quote/belief-obedience-only-he-who-believes-is-obedient-and-only-he-who-is-obedient-believes

Chapter 11: Salvation Vacation

45 https://www.ccel.org/ccel/edwards/works2.vi.xvi.ii.

Chapter 12: Drunk Monkeys

46 https://www.digitalmarketing.org/blog/how-much-time-does-the-average-person-spend-on-social-media

47 https://institutesuccess.com/library/you-are-the-average-of-the-five-people-you-spend-the-most-time-with-jim-rohn-2/

48   https://alltimeshortstories.com/wranglers-and-stranglers

49   The MacArthur Study Bible, English Standard Version (Wheaton, Ill.: Crossway, 2010), 1434; note on Mark 6:5.

Chapter 13: Lights, Camera, Action

50   https://www.success.com/ready-set-go-13-quotes-to-inspire-you-to-take-action

51   Mark Sanborn, *The Fred Factor* (Colorado Springs, CO: Waterbrook Press, 2004).

52   https://www.edisonmuckers.org/thomas-edison-quotes/

53   https://blog.42courses.com/home/2019/12/10/colin-powells-40-70-rule

54   https://www.crosswalk.com/faith/spiritual-life/inspiring-quotes/20-powerful-quotes-from-charles-spurgeon.html

55   Story told by John Maxwell, John Maxwell, *The 15 Invaluable Laws of Growth* (New York: Center Street Pub. 2012) 11.

56   Steve Siebold, *Secrets of the World Class: Turning Mediocrity Into Greatness* (Naperville, Ill.: Simple Truths, 2009), 6.

Chapter 14: SMARTER Goals

57   G. T. Doran (1981). "There's A SMART Way to Write Management Goals and Objectives." *Management Review*, Vol. 70, Issue 11, pgs. 35-36

58   Michael Hyatt *Your Best Year Ever, A Five Step Plan For Achieving Your Best Year* (Grand Rapids, Michigan: Baker Books, 2018).

59   https://leadershipnow.com/visionquotes2.html

60   https:// www.crossway.org/articles/infographic-you-can-read-more-of-the-bible-than-you-think

61   *Your Best Year Ever*, 137.

62   Ibid, 140

63   https://quotefancy.com/quote/7281/Antoine-de-Saint-Exup-ry-A-goal-without-a-plan-is-just-a-wish

64 https://www.forbes.com/sites/markmurphy/2018/04/15/neuroscience-explains-why-you-need-to-write-down-your-goals-if-you-actually-want-to-achieve-them/#33d68e727905

65 Brian Buffini, *The Emigrant Edge* (New York: Howard Books, 2017), 201.

66 Jim Collins and Morten T. Hansen, *Great by Choice* (New Yor: Harper Collins, 2011), 65.

67 https://thenewstack.io/code-n00b-ol-ninety-ninety

68 *Brian Buffini Show* podcast 187, "I Can, I Will, I Believe" with Beverly Buffini

Chapter 15: Urim and Thummim: How to Discover God's Will for Your Life

69 George Sweeting, *How to Discover the Will of God* (Chicago: Moody Bible Institute, 1975), 17.

70 Henry Blackaby and Claude King, *Experiencing God: Knowing and Doing the Will of God* (Nashville: B&H Publishing Group, 2008), 39.

71 Leslie D. Weatherhead, *The Will of God* (Nashville: Festival Books/Abington, 3rd Printing, 1977), 47.

73 https://www.inspiringquotes.us/author/6552-henrietta-mears

74 J. Oswald Sanders, *Every Life Is A Plan of God: Discovering His Will for Your Life* (Grand Rapids: Discovery House, 1992), 109.

75 Blackaby, 174

76 https://www.christianquotes.info/quotes-by-author/phillips-brooks-quotes/

77 C. Mark Corts, *The Caring Christian* (Winston Salem, NC: Sharelife, 1990) 80.

78 https://www.preceptaustin.org/the_will_of_god/john_wesley

79 https://www.georgemuller.org/devotional/how-i-ascertain-the-will-of-god

80 https://billygrahamlibrary.org/6-steps-on-finding-gods-will

81 Henry Blackaby and Claude King, *Experiencing God: Knowing and Doing the Will of God* (Nashville: B&H Publishing Group, 2008).

Chapter 16: SHAPE

82 https:// davidjeremiah.blog/what-it-means-to-be-clay-in-the-hands-of-the-potter/

83 Some of the material of this chapter is adapted from Saddleback Church's Class 301: Discovering My SHAPE for Ministry.

84 https:// goexplorethebible.com/wp-content/uploads/2018/03/DOC-Spiritual-Gifts-Survey.pdf

85 Erik E. Rees, *SHAPE* (Grand Rapids, MI, 2006).

86 From Class 301: Discovering My SHAPE for Ministry.

Chapter 17: Abiding in Christ

87 https://everydaypower.com/george-washington-carver-quotes/

88 https:/ www.crosswalk.com/devotional/insights-from-bill-bright/the-exchanged-life-dec-26.html

89 https://www.wholesomewords.org/missions/biotaylor11.html

Chapter 18: Living Water

90 www.earthobservatory.nasa.gov

91 Lloyd John Ogilvie sermon "Two Thirds Is Not Enough."

92 https://www.cslewisinstitute.org/Power_From_Keep_In_Step_With_The_Spirit

93 https://www.crosswalk.com/devotinals/today-s-insight-july-4-2013.html

94 https://www.tech21century.com/the-human-brain-is-loaded-daily-with-34gb-of-information

95 https://www.azquotes.com/quote/1072564

96 https://www.umcdiscipleship.org/resources/history-of-hymns-trust-and-obey

97 Wayne Grudem, *Systematic Theology* (Grand Rapids MI: Zondervan, 1994), 765.

Chapter 19: Ziklag

98 https://www.bobsredmill.com/bobs-way/meet-bob-and-charlee-moore

99 https://christianindex.org/20151015-weight-lifter-paul-anderson/ RonF.Hale

100 https://www.allchristianquotes.org/index.php?v=page&c=topics&s=6670&l=Tell/Lutzer

Chapter 20: Rebar

101 https://www.spurgeon.org/resource-library/sermons/quiet-musing/#flipbook/

102 Brendon Burchard, *High Performance Habits* (New York: Hay House, 2017) 104.

103 https://newsroom.hobbylobby.com/corporate-background/

104 Taken from David Green, *More than a Hobby* (Nashville: Thomas Nelson, 2005).

105 Jack Canfield, *The Success Principles* (New York: Harper Collins, 2005) 173.

106 https://canadaehx.com/2020/06/28/the-marathon-of-hope/

107 https:// www.healthycommunitieshealthyfuture.org/learnthefacts/economic-costs-of-obesity/

108 https://www.christianitytoday.com/biblestudies/bible-answers/theology/what-does-he-asks-us-to-be-holy.html?start=2

109 https://www.heysigmund.com/the-science-of-gratitude/KarenYoung

110 Charlotte Bronte, *Shirley*, (New York, Penguin Classic ed. 2005)

www.ingramcontent.com/pod-product-compliance
Lightning Source LLC
LaVergne TN
LVHW041905070526
838199LV00051BA/2493